The Guilt Cage

Housewives and a Decade of
Liberation

Suzanne Lowry

ELM TREE BOOKS

Elm Tree Books: London

First published in Great Britain 1980
by Elm Tree Books/Hamish Hamilton Ltd
90 Garden House, 57–59 Long Acre, London WC2E 9JZ

Copyright © 1980 by Suzanne Lowry

British Library Cataloguing in Publication Data

Lowry, Suzanne
    The guilt cage.
    1. Housewives – Great Britain
    2. Feminism – Great Britain – History
    I. Title
    301.41′2   HQ1593
    ISBN 0–241–10293–6

Printed in Great Britain by
Willmer Brothers Limited, Rock Ferry, Merseyside

Contents

Acknowledgements

First I should like to thank all the women who took time and trouble to talk to me, or to my assistant Fiona Malcolm, about their lives and ideas. Some are quoted directly in the book; many more are not, but without their thoughts it certainly would never have been written.

I am grateful to my friends and colleagues. Katharine Whitehorn, Jill Tweedie, Mary Stott, Lyn Owen, Barty Phillips, Hilary Laurie, Dorothy Gharbaoui, Jane McLoughlin and Deborah Singmaster were especially helpful and sympathetic.

I am particularly indebted to Patricia Mann and J. Walter Thompson Limited for their help with the chapters on advertising, and to Gill Vine of the National Housewives Register. Thanks too, to my agent Brian Stone, who pushed me into writing a book in the first place and encouraged me so much on the many occasions when I decided to give up.

I am Margot, housewife, mother, waking to the world
I have made; a warm and homely world in which others
grow if not myself. How nice! But something lingers after
sleep, some sense of sorrow, apprehension. What is it? Am
I in mourning for myself, lost somewhere long ago,
drowned in the sea of other people's demands, a family's
expectations?

Fay Weldon, *Remember Me* 1976

Introduction: In The Second Place

She is my goods, my chattels, she is my house, my household
stuff, my fields, my barn, my horse, my ox, my ass, my anything . . .

The Taming of the Shrew ACT IV Scene II

Who can find a virtuous woman? For her price is above rubies.
The heart of her husband doth safely trust her, so that he shall
have no need of spoil. She is like the merchant's ships she
bringeth her food from afar. She perceiveth that her mer-
chandise is good; her candle goeth not out by night. She looketh
well to her household and does not eat the bread of idleness.

Proverbs 31

It was Mr Micawber, the feckless optimist, who said that 'in
families not regulated by woman in the lofty character of Wife,
accidents may be expected with confidence.' Now Dickens,
Micawber's creator, was a great chronicler of family accidents,
a great evoker of pity for the deserted, helpless and deprived,
and had plenty of Victorian idealism about the perfect woman.

But although his view of the horrific substructures of his
society veered between anger and sentimentality, Dickens was
also capable of irony. He knew that the perfect woman *was* an
ideal, not a reality, and that accidents happened in the face of
the most dedicated and virtuous creatures. He knew too, that,
although a family might be 'regulated' by a wife, it was ruled,
or misruled by a man. His was the kingdom, the power and the
money, seemingly for-ever and ever.

Things have changed, of course, but Dickens would not find
the social organization of our world totally unrecognizable. In
the Britain of the late twentieth century more than half the

adult female population is at work outside the home but an even larger percentage is still hard at work inside it as well, as caring for a family. The marriage rate may be declining, but almost all girls and women under thirty say they want to marry; those who do, go into it with some version of the old mirage of 2.2 children, a house in the country and a loving tender man to provide for them, shimmering before their eyes through the white gauze of their bridal veil. (If you think this kitsch image is an invention, remember that more than £170m was spent on wedding feasts in 1978, according to a survey by *Wedding Day* magazine.) The divorce rate is rising too, of course, but many divorcees remarry in, if you like, a redoubled effort to find happiness. The legally bound couple, for all the trendy examples to the contrary, is still the rock upon which our society is built, and the success of a woman is still measured by, first, her ability to catch a man and marry him and, second, how she performs in the 'lofty character of wife': in other words what kind of home she keeps for her husband and children, how she serves them with food, sex, comforts and, above all, her time, her availability.

There is a good chance that she may be a teacher or a factory worker or (very rarely) managing director of her own company on the side, but the inference usually is that it is the woman's own superpowers of organization that enable her to combine the two roles – and in any crisis, even the man's unemployment, it is assumed that the domestic one would be the last to go. Recent research indicates that many young people these days enter marriage with high ideals of forming the perfect partnership, vowing to share and shoulder everything equally. But, especially after the arrival of the first child, the ancient patterns emerge, and there is little sign that husbands, even those who are prepared to become more involved with their children by changing nappies and administering nocturnal bottles, are assuming any of the real burdens of domesticity. And the chief of these is simply *being there*.

So, caught in the midst of modern debates about women's rights, equal pay and, perennially, 'who-will-look-after-the-children-if-you-don't', is the housewife. She is wooed by politicians at election times in her role as wife, the household regulator. But her individual demands, for, say, adequate day care for the under fives, are ignored. She is studied and importuned and beatified by the advertising industry, again in her role as arch consumer. But finished advertisements take little account of what the woman they are selling to really wants, or what she is really like. She is exhorted to fight all this by her feminist sisters (who may also of course be housewives) while she is loved, or resented or neglected (or all of the above) by her husband.

This is a book about how some of these British women see *themselves*, about how they are perceived (and in some cases manipulated) by others. It is about the gap between image and reality, and how one feeds the other so that it is often difficult to separate the two with any clarity. Just as it is not always clear in a television commercial who is a 'real' housewife – Mrs X from Brandstown, endorsing a product she has actually used – and who is a good actress portraying the stereotype.

It is still the use of the 'housewife' label that most distinguishes women from men. That is true whether it is adopted with pride as the fulfilment of a dream, or with apologies and resentment, or regret for another dream abandoned. For instance, it is quite possible to examine the differences between a male engineer and a female engineer. The most remarkable thing about the latter will be that she is one of so very few; the most remarkable thing about the former may be that he is several kilos heavier than the lady. But in the end, after all the sexist jokes have been cracked, it will come down to a judgement about how well each of them does the *same* job. Real inequality, and the consequent discrimination, sets in when the female is questioned about her domestic commitments.

Even the woman's child-bearing abilities do not open such a gulf between a man and a woman as does her adherence, whether by choice or under duress, to the role of superservant. Housewifery is the X factor, the third dimension, for which women are prepared from childhood, and develop when they marry. Single or divorced women, who may be performing many of the same tasks as the married, rarely, if ever, describe themselves as housewives. The term implies the presence, whether shadowy or overbearing, of a man; a protector and possessor. He is her status symbol and she is his, by unjust exchange one to the other

3

given. Many women of course make the bargain joyfully, only to find that it is at bottom a dreary and demeaning one. Many through personal courage and determination learn to make it work; many more simply learn to 'accept' it. Those whose husbands are successful may enjoy the reflected glory; those married to failures may relish the role of prop and comforter.

Being a housewife gives a woman a mask, it *is* a protection; even her own name disappears. There is a secretiveness, a pride in appearances that makes public complaining difficult and keeps nosy parkers out. One woman, who has now been divorced for many years and is a great success in her own right, asked if it had been difficult to get housewives to talk frankly about themselves: 'When I was living in the country with the children and my husband was going off all the time, I was as miserable as hell but I would *never* have admitted it.' She is right, there is a great investment in saving face: so much so that the Marriage Guidance Council says that by the time people come to them with their problems things have often reached an irretrievable stage and they find themselves handing out divorce counselling instead of help with the marriage.

There are those campaigners who seek to solve the conundrum in a sweeping way by declaring that *all* women, even the Queen, are housewives; there are those who want the very word abolished, and along with it the family structure of which it is the lynch pin. There are others who cling to the 'tradition' of housewifery and would like to see all of us (or at least as many as can find husbands) back in the purdah of the kitchen, the nursery and the bedroom, appearing in public only as the decorative appendage of a man, or possibly to perform charitable works.

I chose to write this book now because it is just a little over ten years since what Germaine Greer called 'the second feminist wave' (female suffragism being the first) burst upon Britain. Her book *The Female Eunuch* appeared in 1970. The same year saw the appearance of Eva Figes' *Patriarchal Attitudes*. Two years later the feminist magazine *Spare Rib* was launched. Only a few years before this and much other activity, the word 'liberation' would have evoked an image of Allied troops marching through France in 1945, rather than a resurgence of the monstrous regiment of women. I hoped to find out what ten years of feminist discussion, action and inaction had done to the grass skirts of Britain, and to see how the thinking of some of those who rode the crest of the 'second wave' had changed.

It is a relatively simple matter to list the 'achievements' such as the anti-discrimination legislation of the mid-seventies; much more difficult to measure private change. A sense that the old order of things is in a time of trial and flux persists. It is fostered by the kind of 'progressive' newspaper I have worked for – the *Guardian* and, latterly, the *Observer* – because they provide some limited platform for the most articulate (if not always the most extreme) advocates of change, and some small forum for arguments about the issues that are of prime importance to women, whatever view they take of them. The tax system, child care and child rearing, wife battering, rape and abortion are some examples.

Other signals run counter to this. When magazines with circulations larger than that of the *Guardian* and the *Observer* and the *Sunday Times* put together, can conduct surveys which show that girls reaching maturity now, still dream the impossible dream of husband, two-and-a-half children and roses round the door forever, or which demonstrate that women may be unsatisfied with their sex lives but are quite content with their housework; when advertisers continue to sell to women by holding up an ideal image of a wholesome, capable, ever smiling stereotype for her to identify with, it surely indicates some gulf between the 'leaders' or 'spokespersons' of women and their constituency.

If such a gap does exist, whose fault is it? Are women themselves to blame, or the various media engaged in selling to, and preaching at them?

The women in this book are on the whole described by themselves; they are tagged as housewives because they themselves see themselves as such or have 'accepted' the job description, however reluctantly. Each uses the word from her own standpoint. But in general a housewife is taken to mean a woman who is married, probably but not necessarily, with children. She may or may not do other work. The position of single women, whether unmarried or divorced, is examined only in that it is

5

inevitably affected by society's overwhelming devotion to the housewife norm.

I wanted to understand why it is so difficult, even for women who recognize the restrictions of the housewife's lot, to give it all up and strive, as the feminists so cogently urge, for a more independent life, a more broadly-based community in which to rear our children. There are obvious reasons, such as fear, lack of money and loss of confidence: even quite highly-qualified women who have not been working for years regard even the idea of going for a job interview with terror. Is male dominance to blame? Or is it in the end the domestic power base women are unwilling to relinquish? A housewife's whole life may belong to her husband and her children, but she in return has full control of a large part of their daily lives. She can determine what they are, at least within certain bounds, as she chooses their socks and their menus and irons their shirts and decides that the sitting room should be painted green. It is an illusion, but a comforting one and provides, at least for a while, a sense of security and a human hold on *people* rather than things not readily available to women anywhere else.

Having domestic control gives a woman a spurious power over the man, as all the time-honoured jokes about nagging and hen-pecking wives illustrate. The woman is the moral guardian of the family and the man, while accepting this authority, can, at the same time, kick against it in good naughty boy tradition – beating the woman up once in a while (mentally or physically or both), just to remind her who is *really* boss. Since 'liberation', the 'jokes' have gained a new element: a man will now preface his anti-woman cliches with the phrase 'I may be a male chauvinist pig, but . . .'

Joking apart, why so many men continue to want their wives to be housewives and nothing else is easy to see. Having a wife at home is, as has been often remarked, similar to having a super secretary whose time is all yours and who gives you more besides. It is a curious psychological fact, a kind of domestic offshoot of Parkinson's Law that housework, more than any other labour, expands to fill the time in which the doer is available. In other words, it can take a whole morning to collect the car from the garage, or change a shirt or go to the shoemakers. Women drift around supermarkets as if in a dream. Tradespeople are in on this and serve women with no sense of urgency. Many a working woman would be glad to have someone performing these tasks for her on a daily unpaid basis. In America there is now at least one enterprising woman who is offering such a service on a commercial basis with a company called Rent-A-Wife. Many of her clients are working women and, needless to say, she is making a bomb.

In many households in Britain (although it was supposed to be a working class tradition) it is not uncommon for the wife to be the 'regulator' to such an extent that the man hands her his wage packet each week or salary cheque each month and she doles it out again and pays the rent and other bills. That doesn't make her rich or free; it merely means that the husband is getting a free banking and accountancy service as well as everything else.

There has been no shortage in the past ten years of writing and talking by British feminists, but somehow it has been (after *The Female Eunuch*, which was in any case written by an Australian) the American works that have had most sensational impact. Apart from Betty Friedan's *The Feminine Mystique*, which uncovered the authentic unsugared voice of the American wife and Mom as long ago as 1963, and, later, Kate Millet's *Sexual Politics*, there has been a plethora of novels which have had avowedly feminist intent but whose authors have explored the notion of sexual, rather than domestic, liberation. Erica Jong, prophetess of the multiple orgasm, Lisa Alther, author of *Kinflicks*, lead this field.

Betty Friedan's astonishing and frightening book was researched and written in the days before consciousness raising and sisterhood, before dungarees and unpermed hair (feminists came late to the pseudo afro frizz as a badge of solidarity and asexuality). Friedan identified 'the problem that has no name' – no name, because at that time neither therapists, doctors nor the women themselves had any way of labelling the terrible emptiness at the heart of housewifely life in the suburbs of the richest country on earth. There they sat at the mouth of the post war American consumer cornucopia, apparently chief beneficiaries

7

of the American dream's realization. And yet, and yet . . . wasn't there something more?

Betty Friedan listened carefully to the words of the women who were little more than 'furniture in their own homes', and warned of what would happen to all of us, men, women and especially children, if women went on living the half-life of the housewife-dependent, suffocating both her husband and her children while being suffocated herself. Friedan attributes the passivity of so many American children of that generation of women to the fact that their mothers, hung up on the false mystique of femininity, never matured, never realized their own identity.

Nothing better or more comprehensive has been written about women caught in the web of affluence and domestic oppression. *The Feminine Mystique* is still sold in some editions with the tag 'the bestseller that ignited women's liberation'. But Friedan was not quite alone. Joan Baez was already a veteran, singing 'Babe I'm Gonna Leave You' as far back as 1959. The whole temper of the age was changing. The Vietnam war shook the passive youth into protest, and love, peace and sisterhood became the causes of the sixties and early seventies. (Talk now, on the edge of a new decade, is of backlash and regression.)

All this, remember, was in America – a distant display of fireworks. Because of the common language and a wealth of common concerns and experience, the 'special relationship' between Britain and America has been over-estimated. The British 'feminine mystique' was the same, but different. True, there was a surburban ideal, an effort to persuade women who had taken responsible roles in the war to return to domesticity and so they did. But there was also an old class system, a new health service and above all, no such uniform affluence as was experienced in America. (The British statistics about the lack of bathrooms and dearth of dishwashers are oft quoted derisively by American commentators.)

Not surprising, then, that women's liberation in America was instantly a commercial success. *Ms* magazine, for instance, was immediately taken up by the advertisers, adapting their copy as they saw the new direction the consuming woman's thought was taking. (Here, *Spare Rib* has had to fight hard for survival.)

The American women's movement may have done little to help the poor woman of the US – but, at a glossier level, women are now big business. Most of the so-called new 'women's films' have been no more than old fashioned romantic dramas inhabited by very good actresses such as Jane Fonda and Shirley Maclaine, fed up with the era of balls and beefcake versus tits and bum.

Back in Britain, to say that something is 'feminist' or a 'women's' book/movie/exhibition is still, according to some feminist writers, the kiss of derision.This has a lot to do with the image of feminism in this country and the kind of rotten egg abuse that men (and some women) have thrown at women prepared to get up on campaign platforms. The hard-won success of two women's publishing imprints (Virago and The Women's Press) is helping to change that. But on the whole women writers, even when they write about women sensitively and with social purpose, dodge the feminist tag.

What has happened in the last ten years is that a wealth of *documentary* literature about and for women has appeared. There are new guides and directories to every aspect of a woman's life – information about her body, her children and her rights on an unprecedented scale – and this has had a tremendous influence on the way some women talk about themselves, and on their confidence. This has been particularly striking in the case of working class women, many of whom have been liberated by the simple possibility of raising a healthy family of a chosen size.

But the fact remains, our voices are nowhere near the level of stridency or effectiveness heard in America, and in France and Italy. Do we suffer from the British disease of complacency? Is it defeatism? Or ignorance? Or an inbred talent for self deprecation? Are women in Britain scared or lazy or both?

Is there, perhaps, a strain in British women's thinking that American women have shuffled off or have never had? Again and again in interviews for this book, a woman would voice a mild complaint and then remind herself that it was after all her own fault, her own look out to keep herself 'busy and happy'. There is a great readiness among women here to take responsibility for their own emotional difficulties which puts them both a step ahead and a step behind their American sisters, who seem all too ready to blame men in general, and the man sleeping next to them in particular, for their woes.

The British housewife's reluctance to complain (stiff upper lip if you like) can mean danger when she is really in trouble. But such self control *could* be the root of a new independent spirit, which could grow to allow women to regain power over themselves.

One new breed that seemed to emerge from the consciousness raising of the sixties was what was known as the captive wife (see Hannah Gavron's book of that name): the graduate who *might* have had a great career, but who didn't because she got married. Nappy changing and short change could not satisfy her; she *knew* she was more intelligent than her husband and than most other men, but had neither the will nor the opportunity to prove it. She was not quite rich enough to engage the kind of help that would set her free and yet not poor enough to *have* to do a job and bring in some extra money whether she liked it or not. And, of course, there was the tax system; because of her husband's earning she'd be left with next to nothing anyway. Better to sit around with others in the same boat picking the world to pieces and dreading the moment when at a dinner party someone would turn to her and say, 'What do *you* do?'

These were, believe it or not, the inheritors of the suffragettes, they were the women who got education and franchise and sold it for a mess of domesticity. They gained an empire but didn't know how to lose a role. Some solved their problems by living up to the dizzy hen image, so perpetrated by newspapers and magazines in the fifties and sixties, of the crazy, funny madcap woman who managed to do a bit of everything and yet be loving and ultra feminine too. Katharine Whitehorn wrote for a whole generation of middle class women when she owned up to being a slut and made it forever after respectable to fish yesterday's knickers out of the laundry box. Alongside the dizzies came the sombre-faced, dispossessed women whose marriages and *amour propre* could not survive their own disaffection: divorced, or just determined, they became the first housewife-feminist activists.

Because this group and its subdivisions has been and is so vocal, and concerns itself so much with the domestic, mothering role of women, there is quite a lot in this book about them, and what has happened to them ten or fifteen years on. There is discussion of the media reflection of their thinking, and interviews with women who *should* have been most affected by ten years of feminism – thirty-five year olds, perhaps with a couple of children. It would seem that they are still caught between wanting the 'new' freedoms brought by independent work and sexuality, but are all the same firmly harnessed to the chimera of happy family life – a man, children, a nice house and sexual fealty.

The working class women (and perhaps it is one answer to the question of why feminism has no united voice in Britain to say that women are still, except in small metropolitan pockets, rigidly divided by the class system) have a different mythology, based in the bitter history of the Industrial Revolution and from the hard years in the first half of this century. The precious vote did little to help those working women and only now are they finding a trade union voice distinct from that of the men.

As housewives they are more dedicated than their middle class sisters, their race memory is not of servants but of a grinding necessity to go out to work, not at a career but at anything, simply to make ends almost meet. The rewards of staying at home to look after the children may at first seem sweeter to them, but the destruction of the old urban communities and the extended families have placed many of these women in isolation too terrible to bear. The young mother who jumped from the top of her high rise apartment block clutching her baby is a tragic symbol of their despair.

I have not attempted, in spite of this sketchy preamble, to give a detailed historical analysis of why we have arrived at this pass, or why it is that the women of the Western World find themselves in such strange gadget-ridden servitude. Ann Oakley did that very fully in her excellent *Housewife* (Penguin 1974) – although I don't go all the way with her idealization of women's lot in the seventeenth and eighteenth century pre-Industrial days. Germaine Greer gave her historical view in *The Female Eunuch*.

Nor do I wish to seem to put down any woman, except perhaps she who, as Erin Pizzey once put it, 'sells out for a three piece suite.' I don't believe it is usually as simple as that anyway.

The compromise women are forced to make is more binding, more complex. I wanted to look at the nature of that compromise and try to uncover a little of the real woman behind the perfect imitation whose image hovers forever before our eyes, on a million hoardings, news stands and TV screens.

Part One

Housewives, the Media and the Message

Fundamental Soup Values

The gynolatry of our civilization is written large upon its face; upon hoardings, cinema screens, television, newspapers, magazines, tins, packets, cartons, bottles, all consecrated to the reigning deity, the female fetish.

Germaine Greer, *The Female Eunuch*, 1970

Why is it never said that the really crucial function, the really important role that women serve as housewives is to *buy more things for the house?*

Betty Friedan, *The Feminine Mystique*, 1963

If there is anyone casting an ever-beady eye on what women in general and housewives in particular are doing and thinking and tending towards, it is a manufacturer of consumer goods. Or rather, that high priest of our culture, his advertising agent.

There are 306 advertising agencies registered with the Institute of Practitioners in Advertising (IPA) in this country, many of them branches or subsiduaries of American or multi-national companies. There are several hundreds more small or oddball outfits also extant. Through them manufacturers spent £204 millions in 1978 on promoting household and leisure goods alone, although in fact advertising agencies now help to sell everything from soap powder to the prime minister. If any innocent or sceptical reader still needs convincing of the skill, success and influence of advertising men and women, and the medium they animate, they should take note that in the last ten years in Britain, election campaign managers of the old fashioned 'roadie' variety have taken second place to advertising consultants and 'image' advisers. The Americans started it – in earnest from the time that a 5 o'clock shadow did for Nixon's election chances when he faced Kennedy in 1960. Now, the pitch of the voice, the turn of phrase, the closeness of the shave and the tightness of the perm are subtleties which may seem to be the essence of triviality, but can, all agree, be deployed to persuade us to vote yea or nay.

In short, image in prime time is of prime importance. Politicians have borrowed techniques which have proved successful on the pulses of customers in search of the best margarine. The media image of a politician, even though he or she may be selling policies and ideology, rather than Rice Krispies or peanuts, is important roughly in the same way that the image of the housewife endorsing this or that soap powder is vital. It must strike a chord in the mind, or the subconscious, or the race memory of the beholder, which will not be loud enough to jar or alarm, nor quiet or dreary enough to bore. Like baby bear's porridge it must be just right, so that the potential customer will eat it all up, if not swallow it whole, and rush out and buy, or vote as the case may be.

Hitting this chord without jarring *is* a kind of genius and leads to power and riches for the one who achieves it and whomsoever he or she represents. Getting it wrong is an expensive disaster.

So, it is scarcely to be wondered at that extreme care, many thousands of pounds, and many more thousands of men and women hours, are expended in attempting to get it right. 'Creative' may be the keynote word in the advertising business, but caution is the key. It is necessary not only to project an image that is eye-catching and persuasive; it must also be acceptable to as many people as possible. And to those people to whom it is *not* acceptable, it must at least say something, be explicable and recognizable. Hence the much-hated but persistent housewife stereotype.

Not many women I know like to think of themselves at the kitchen sink or scrubbing the floor. But whether or not they do housework every day, or refuse on principle to do it at all, they all know what it *means*. Mum in the kitchen is still at the centre of our dreams and nightmares, if not about ourselves, then about others. Thus, so many of the women I talked with in the course of preparing this book would say 'yes, I am a housewife, but I'm not typical. Talk to so and so, because she *is* – she bakes her own bread, and runs the local playgroup, her house is perfect, she loves her children ...' The typicality can take any number of forms. When I followed this trail, I would find that so and so had some other paragon in the corner of her mind's eye whom *she* thought truly expressed an ideal of housewifery – the perfect custodian of our daily bread and daily peace of mind. She didn't necessarily wish to *be* this perfect neighbour, or even to copy her, but she knew she was there.

There are those career women and feminists (not necessarily the same people) who totally reject the housewifely image and abjure the role, and who are angered by its omnipresence. Certainly, viewed realistically, it is both unfair and untrue to depict women in this way: it isn't like that, not quite, even at best or worst. But a kind of moral nostalgia, a need for reassurance that we are still protected by the way we and life were, calls up a response. And, we are further assured, sells the product.

The purist objection to the stereotyped images of the housewife – the spick and span, coiffed and coffee-drinking, all-smiling all-servicing Mum is roughly the same one as that advanced against soft porn. It demeans any human being to present him or her in sub-human form, to show them only in terms of role or body definition, and not as individuals, complete with soul peeking through. Thus, if a woman is shown naked, moulded into plastic 'provocative' perfection, it tends to encourage men to continue to think of women as sex objects, and to continue to behave accordingly.

Likewise, if you present a woman in a kitchen serving her family, as the perfect all-weather provider, addicted to washing-up liquid and obsessed by clean surfaces, you encourage men to continue to think of that as her place and role, while women themselves are reinforced in a role they may have doubts about and resentment against.

To answer both the anti-sex object and anti-household slave cases, a version of the innocent savage theory is often advanced. If women have beautiful bodies they *enjoy* showing them off, they enjoy arousing men's lust; if a woman has domestic ability, if she is married and finds herself in the kitchen and is making the best of it, then she is happier that way, that is where she has chosen to be. Anything else would be 'upsetting' to her.

Most of the women interviewed for this book, and many others with whom I discussed the subject, denied that they were influenced by advertising either on television or in magazines, except in that it made them familiar with product names (which, of course, is half the advertiser's battle). Among twenty-five women questioned directly, only three admitted that they regularly consciously tried something new after watching advertisements. They added, however, that if they bought the product and disliked it or found it wanting, their scepticism about advertising would be increased, and they would not buy it again. All but two of these women – and they lived in the country and shopped in old fashioned grocery stores – said that they *were* influenced by the way products were displayed in a supermarket. If something looked attractive they were tempted, even if they hadn't seen it advertised elsewhere, or thought of buying before.

No one much liked the image of women shown using the products in television commercials; some were stung by the stereotyped, plastic view of their kind. But they didn't, except in the case of those who had worked out a clear feminist objection, think it was terribly important. The anodyne, even bland, presentation of the housewife on television, may not be accurate or very acceptable, but it is not strident enough to offend the casual viewer. The general thinking among women, as among admen, appeared to be product-orientated. 'If I like something, if it works, and I can afford it, I go on buying it.'

It is curious that the explosion in consumer advertising, which is so often blamed for the abuse and denigration of women, has happened alongside women's emancipation and increasing economic freedom.

As the second half of this century rolled away from the bleak post war years, through the difficult fifties, and into the now mythical, indulgent, money-spinning sixties, women were offered more domestic aids, more and more products and machines to add to their efficient performance in the role they were starting to dissent from, question, and split with other roles. Wives had always been the budgeters, the shoppers, the domestic managers, what Alec Douglas Home could still, if quaintly, call, 'housekeepers' in 1964. At the beginning of this century, they were making almost everything for use in the home, including their own candles; selling and promotion was done over the counter or in the shop window. Buying, for most, was a question of necessity, not indulgence. By the 1960s, women were flicking an increasing number of switches, and the marketplace had moved from the high street to the sitting room. Choice could be made before ever crossing the shop threshold.

Post war advertising, before commercial television, was confined in Britain to papers, magazines and hoardings; it was both cosy and perfectionist in its depiction of housewives. There was at the time a great national drive to get women back into the home and although that was scarcely the advertisers' fault, they did a lot to foster it. Motherhood and homecrafts were paramount; aprons and overalls to the fore. What is more, the tasks had to be performed to a rigidly high standard if the woman was to avoid the censure of her neighbours or her husband or both.

Then arose the bright young 'modern housewife' – a bit scatty and wild and likely to be getting into madcap scrapes, but loving and sensible and motherly at heart. She was just a bit slimmer, perkier, and outward-looking than her Mum. She was indefatigably middle class, in an Enid Blyton sixth form kind of way. Katie of Oxo was her most perfect expression; the head girl.

The fact that Katie is no longer with us is often cited by advertising people as a good example of how their medium moves with the times. Patricia Mann, an associate senior director of the J. Walter Thompson agency in Britain, pointed to the new ambiguity in the presentation of women : they may be presented in a domestic role, collecting kids, rushing to finish the shopping, but there is no way of telling that the rest of their day is not spent in an office or some other place of employment. And since, remember, half the married women in this country do a job of some kind, that is surely a fair reflection.

On the other hand some of the best-known and most successful campaigns have changed little since modern-style advertising began. Persil soap powder, which has been on the market since 1909, for instance. Thirty years ago the line was 'Persil Washes Whiter – And It Shows.' The slogan was accompanied by a man, woman, or child in a perfect Persil-white shirt/frock, striding past a guilty and horror-stricken mirror image wearing a grey garment that had been immersed in some other, inferior, product. Now the pitch is softer; Persil still washes whiter, but these days it *cares*. As one advertising executive carefully explained to me, people no longer feel so guilty about not getting things white enough to match up to Mrs Jones's laundry standards. But they *do* place enormous value on loving and devotion to family; a clean wash is soft as well as white, to express love as well as virtue.

Thus, the creators of a new campaign for Knorr soup in 1978, pitched towards 'the kind of woman who buys or is thinking of buying packet soups – the younger C-1s in the socio-economic scale', were seeking to evoke 'fundamental soup values' in their advertisement. These, as you might guess, have a lot to do with warmth and hearth-and-home love and life style and will, it is assumed, also have a lot to do with the C-1 housewife's image of what she ought to be aiming for.

Before deciding on a final scenario, the agency, J. Walter Thompson, consulted a panel of housewives. This is a routine part of the research process for any advertisement. The women are chosen from the 'target group' according to their predicted interest in the product; they meet either at the agency offices or at one of their own homes. Judie Lannon, a director of JWT and the head of their research unit, explained that for the Knorr campaign they held four or five such discussion groups. 'We showed them the versions of proposed advertisement, talked through the alternatives with them and asked them which they liked. The response was interesting and very realistic.'

The kind of comment forthcoming was usually drawn from the women's own experience. They would say that children didn't like packet soups, or that he (the husband) wouldn't have it. They thought that one version made the children look too greedy, and they offered hints about the casting.

This product had a slight exoticism because of the name, but it also had to appear down to earth. The woman using it had to be 'not a scrubber but not posh; she had to emanate a vague mass of C-oneishness' said Judie Lannon. That formula means nice hair, a fresh face, unmade up looking, nice to know, but not passive. An ordinary woman, never in fancy clothes which the women in the target group would find laughable. What is more, advertisements of this kind don't work, reported Judie Lannon, if the children are shown as too rude, or if the housewife is shown as stupid or gullible or waiting for approval.

In the end the Knorr ad was a gentle joke at the expense of the product's name: K-norr, K-norman and so on. It was, said Judie Lannon, attention-getting, it took the stereotype and made fun of it. Women were not really expected to identify directly with the housewife portrayed. In the same way, with Mac-Dougall's flour, they showed the kind of woman who might bake her own bread, plump and motherly to evoke the product's value. It's a kind of shorthand; all part of the cliché tradition.

Judie Lannon was well aware of the 'new sense of diversity and individualism' that has characterized women in the last decade. She welcomed the fact that ads spark controversy. After all, 'what is patronizing to one person is sympathetic to another; a joke succeeds with some; fails with others. One woman's pleasure is another's hell.'

But she has looked further back to show just how far advertising has come since the days when the Victorian manufacturers simply made the assumption that they had a product that all women must surely want. 'Technological progress was under way, and the lure of a faster, easier, life was irresistible; an aesthetic announcement was all that was needed.' We will never, she declared, know whether the Edwardian or working class women of the twenties and thirties identified with the advertising of the time or not; but certainly the biggest difference between ads of that time and now is the tone of voice. Then 'the tone was the lofty voice of progress and authority; the path was laid for a better life and it was the responsibility of manufacturers to educate rather than simply to inform.' These advertisers told housewives how to do housework, how to feed their children and how to make their husbands happy. 'By today's standards the tone is patronizing' said Judie Lannon. 'I suspect that at the time it was considered helpful and sympathetic.' She points to a strange reversal between ads and editorial in women's magazines. Then the ads addressed themselves to the problems of women: 'Drunkenness cured', 'Baby wasting away ?', 'Why acid stomachs are dangerous', and so on. Meanwhile the editorial pages were genteel, and sidestepped such realities, concentrating on etiquette and decorum and romance. 'Nowadays editorial is dealing with the realities while advertisements often sound oddly bland and euphemistic by comparison.'

Judie Lannon was not sure whether it was the arrival of motivation research, 'laying bare the secrets of the female psyche', or simply an increase in women writing for other women, but the advertising of the fifties 'went for the jugular of female vulnerability like no period before or since'. She did not think that any advertising today could so blatantly aim at the social anxieties and insecurities as those for lavatory cleaners and soap powders of thirty or so years ago. 'The motives for a clean bathroom and clean clothes were dealt with head on; no euphemisms here. Standards of cleanliness were paramount and disapproval intolerable; the need for social conformity was very strong.'

Apart from Persil, she recalled the famous Horlicks campaign – a cartoon strip which showed the tragic result of insomnia or insufficient sleep. Sometimes the sufferer was a husband and father, but the majority were hair-raising tales of housewifely failure: 'Too tired to perform household tasks, too tired to be sparkling company to her husband's friends, too exhausted to be the patient and understanding mothers expected by their children.'

By the 1960s things were a bit different. That decade, Judie Lannon pointed out, produced 'the first generation in this century in the West with no childhood recollection of war and its accompanying effects of denial and insecurity ... there was an overwhelming sense that one had more chance than ever to have a better start in life, get a better education and a better job. Compared to the lives of their parents young people saw life as essentially more colourful, more varied, more exciting: in their homes, personal appearance, entertainment and holidays.' And underlying all this positive, optimistic and occasionally rebellious outlook, she said, was the belief in personal freedom. There was also a belief that social class was breaking down. Fashion and cosmetics no longer identified status; sports were open to everyone. There was greater availability of material possessions such as cars, television sets, holidays abroad.

In 1965, fifty-six per cent of households had a washing machine; by 1975 it was seventy-one per cent. Households with central heating had jumped from sixteen per cent to forty-nine per cent, colour television owners or renters from none to forty-five per cent.

By the 1960s advertising researchers were studying the housewife continuously and intensively. A year ago there was a conference in London on Advertising and Marketing to Women. Eileen Cole, the chief executive of Unilever's Research International, tried to explore and evaluate the changes that had taken place in the role, attitude and lifestyles of women in the last ten years. After listing education, legal status and fertility control, she went on to discuss what she saw as probably the most dramatic change in the social situation of women which has ever occurred. 'The whole of the very steep increase in the total labour force in this country between 1951 and 1976 was made up of entry into that market by women. The vast majority were married women – four million of them – and their entry has dramatically changed both the size of the total labour force, and its nature. Seventy per cent of women workers are married, and a quarter of the total work force is made up of married women.' In 1951, she pointed out, these percentages were thirty-eight per cent and eleven per cent respectively.

'It seems fairly straightforward to think of married women going out to work, getting outside interests, outside knowledge and an income of their own . . .' she said, but she warned the change is not without its hazards. Unemployment, for instance, and the concentration of the female labour force on too small a front. 'A larger proportion of women is increasingly employed in cooking and catering and retailing, hairdressing, clerical work, and nursing. And forty-one per cent of the female work force is part time.' She believes, however, that gradually the equal pay battle is being won.

The most fascinating prognostication by Eileen Cole was about what was happening to family and household size. The annual number of marriages, which had been increasing steadily

23

until 1971 fell back by 1976, while the divorce rate (especially since the 1967 Act) has been increasing rapidly :

'The birth rate per woman has fallen away very dramatically from 1960 to 1976 and – although it is too early to absolutely show the later child-bearing pattern of women born in 1950 – the indications are that they have fewer children, spread over a shorter time than their mothers. So, fewer marriages, more divorces, fewer children.

'In the fifteen years between 1961 and 1976 the average household size has fallen from just over 3 to 2.76. This means that the number of one and two parent households has risen from forty-two per cent to fifty-three per cent. By 1982 the proportion of one and two person households will be a staggering sixty per cent. The number of one person households has already risen from twelve per cent to twenty-one per cent and is expected to be thirty per cent of all households by the end of the next decade. And most of them will be women.'

On average, said Eileen Cole, something like twenty to twenty-five years of family life are now being spent without children at home. And the number of one parent families is growing significantly – up by 200,000 to 750,000 in the fifteen years up to 1978. Most of *them* are headed by women. 'For women in situations like this, particularly if they are bringing up a family on their own income, life will be stressful and difficult. For many of their more fortunate sisters the picture is a very different one. Better education, more women working outside the home, fewer children, greater freedom from the constraints of a family spread over a number of years.'

Eileen Cole also pointed to a cultural improvement in women's lives. They travel more, take more interest in holidays, more hold driving licences, they see more of life and the world. 'However – and it is a big however – in gaining work outside the home, they have not succeeded so well in sharing it inside the home, so that many of them effectively have two jobs.'

She was, while going on to examine all this in terms of marketing and advertising, careful to emphasize that no change takes place on its own, and that, while these changes have been going on for women, other changes have been taking place in the economic and social scene generally. 'Inflationary pressure has perhaps meant that more women have wanted to work to balance the family budget. And in manufacturing and retailing there have been dramatic changes which have in themselves affected the social situation of women.' But she did see a number of areas in which the change in women's position *itself* has caused other change, which deeply involved all aspects of marketing. For example, better education means more discrimination in the sense of selectivity : 'If you are involved in market research, you inevitably have a deep respect for the common sense and ability to discriminate of the housewife. But her growing independence and her growing education will mean greater confidence in her own ability in this area. She is likely to buy products and view advertising with a colder, clearer eye than ever before. This does not mean that women do not see themselves as homemakers, nor that they view all advertising which shows them in this role as sexist and discriminating. Nevertheless advertisers who patronize them will need to beware.'

Eileen Cole reckoned that the growing proportion of women living on their own, reasonably financially independent and certain of social independence – that is, feeling themselves perfectly capable of making their own way in the world if they want to – would have their eyes less in-turned to domestic tasks, and more out-turned to living life more fully, whatever this may mean to them as individuals.

But, 'where they have two jobs – inside and outside the home – they will be increasingly interested in consumer capital goods which make life easier (e.g. freezers and micro ovens) and may improve its quality'.

The effects of revolution, as Eileen Cole could see, are hard to measure while it is still going on. But it is essential to remember that the notion of housewifery as an ideal state is very new. The role has in the past been idealized, in the sense that women running a home, mothering children and tending their husbands, keeping the home fires burning against heavy odds, were seen as heroic, and perhaps properly so. But the idealism was chiefly attached to the motherly role and the moral values a good woman was said to enshrine. Agnes at the end of David Copperfield is an inspiration, 'pointing upwards' (her predecessor in David's affections, Dora, was a hopeless, if adorable, housekeeper). The matrons on the First World War posters have no compunction in saying 'Go'. Men were a fair sacrifice; women willing priestesses.

Nobody pretended that the actual domestic work had anything noble or attractive about it. Right up to the Second World War, any household who could afford a servant, often little more than a kept drudge, who in return for a roof and sustenance took on the bleaker kitchen chores – did so. The annals of 'service' are full and fascinating ones; the backs of many a dispossessed female carried the families of the late Industrial Revolution.

Beneath this level lay poverty and martyrdom and disease and death of a kind we cannot now imagine outside the Third World. It is heart-breakingly catalogued in such volumes as Gwen Peember Reeves's *Round About A Pound A Week*, a turn-of-the-century study of working class conditions in South London. Perhaps an even more vivid illustration of what the much maligned welfare state has achieved is contained in *Working Class Wives* by Margery Spring Rice, a study of 1,250 married women based on information collected by the Women's Health Enquiry Committee in the 1930s. The poverty uncovered was horrific. Take, for instance, Mrs B, who lived 'in two rooms in a house over a shop in Bermondsey. She is thirty-nine and has eight children of whom six are living, their ages ranging from twelve to two years; her husband is a carman and gives her £2.4.0 for housekeeping. She says her weekly meals consist of:

Breakfast: bread and margarine, tea
Dinner: "Daily Sketch", or bread and cornbeef
Tea: bread and margarine
Supper: cannot afford them.'

The rent was 7/6 and she didn't feel that the day's work was too hard for her, but 'she doesn't feel well and suffers from faintness and headaches because she is "sun starved". She takes castor oil and lemon for this, and says she cannot afford doctors.'

In the conclusion to this volume of deprivation, the outraged committee members stated roundly that 'all except a very few of the families of whom these women are the mothers and managers, are too poor . . . to buy healthy satisfaction even of

26

their primary needs, food, fuel and light, decent housing and a minimum of clothing and household equipment.'

Things were tough after the war too, but the Welfare State took the edge off the worst poverty and health hazards. Working class women began to emerge from the grim purdah of their home lives which involved a daily round of housework and child care mercifully few women face in Britain today. The balance of their housework and work they may have been doing outside the home did not magically right itself, but life after marriage became less punitive physically.

Very gradually improvement in health and education levels, as well as fertility control, edged these women towards something Margery Spring Rice's committee observed to be utterly out of the reach of the group they studied – fulfilment and some kind of cultural life. Their new asset, spending power, turned them from being simply survivors into that new species of the modern West, consumers.

Meanwhile, in the better suburbs, the post war generation of middle class women were the first of their kind ever to find themselves without servants, or with only minimal paid help. They knuckled down with a will (hadn't their menfolk won the war and wasn't it up to them to win the peace for their children) but, perhaps because the new servants, machines, became available to this group first, it was they who first saw the flaws in this new cosy domestic bliss. Machines don't talk, or take orders and they are difficult to mend; housework, even in a nice house, is drudgery, only visible when it is not performed. Child care, even in a good happy home, can be dangerously lonely. The most expensive and miracle-working Hoover can combine with the most wondrous, adored child to tyrannize their keeper. Waiting for the service man is no fun.

The women whose mothers had really known what drudgery meant were less anxious to knock the new, improved housewife ideal. They made the transition from slave to consumer gladly and were almost grateful for the blandishments of the ad men. Meanwhile their middle class sisters had moved down from managerial level to become the best dressed and educated servants the country has ever known. The captive wife was born.

The great spin-off from this coddled discontent and self waste was, of course, one wing of the new women's movement. And sisterhood: a dawning sense among privileged women that unless they banded together with others like themselves to break the seductively gilded fetters a husband and a family could place around them, the bands would close tighter and tighter and all hope of free flight would be lost.

It has been hard for good hearted men to understand why their wives, upon whom they lavish (they imagine) their hard-earned salaries and wages, resent their gadget-propped comfort. 'What's the matter with you – is there anything you want' is a common cry from an affluent husband, imagining somehow that a new washing machine or a holiday might do the trick.

Part of the trouble is that so many men who do boring, exhausting, even mentally or physically dangerous jobs think they are doing them in order to keep their wives happy and their children safe and to achieve a better 'standard of living for them'. What they don't realize is that they are also requiring the family, and their wives in particular, to live out their own fantasy for them. A move to the country or the outer suburbs may be a man's idea of how to pursue rural bliss or increased status. But he is likely to spend the long daylight hours on trains and behind desks; the hard won good life has to be led vicariously through his other half. The woman, often unknowingly, connives at this and tries hard to live up to the husband's image – all the time spending more and more of his money at the supermarket on products that the advertisers tell her will bring her closer to perfection or freedom, or at least a white wash.

Market researchers talk a lot about the spending power of the housewife. But even for a woman who works it is usually money provided by her husband she is spending, or relying on. While the new machines and higher standards of living generally have lightened a woman's domestic load, the cost has made her even more dependent on the higher-earning male. The woman's money, if she earns any, is often used to maintain the much more expensive and more elaborate technology and property structure of their joint lives. If she left, or if he walked out, in spite of kinder divorce and separation laws, her standard of living is likely to drop away out of reach of a washing machine,

28

or perhaps even central heating. If she keeps them, she may not be able to afford the running costs.

So, although women have undisputed spending power, they don't have income-generating power. The washing machine may be *for* them but it is not usually *theirs* in any secure sense. Since market researchers know more about housewives than anyone outside a sociology department they are well aware of this fact. Is it some kind of recognition of the financial power-base that helps preserve the housewife stereotype in advertising? A woman alone, however confident and discriminating would simply not be able to consume as much as the one who spends for her man. Does the need, in the last analysis, to sell a product rather than give free courses in sociology or consciousness-raising explain why so much of the expensively collected information about marriage, divorce and child-rearing patterns, and women's changing attitudes, is so little reflected in the finished television commercials or posters or magazine ads?

I have given a potted, oversimplified account of how we moved from the pre- and post-war doldrums into the era of the new women's movement and the consumer advertising age. The heroine of this saga has been the housewife, struggling for her family's wellbeing and for her own identity at the same time. She now appears as the new 'ambiguous' woman of the television commercials. She is not always in the cage, nor is she ever quite out of it. She is still shopping, still washing up, cooking, ironing shirts and drinking Nescafé and Lucozade. Only now, as a concession to her growing confidence and independence, there is sometimes a hinted-at other life, beyond the gleaming stainless steel sink, the soft hands and the mentholated smile. Who is this new paragon?

Supermum and The Idiot

Margaret Mead says that there is no job which has not been an all male job in some community, and an all female job in another the only difference is that where men do it, it's regarded as high powered and difficult, and if it's women's work it's a lowly chore. At the rate we're going the only job left to carry high prestige as a male exclusive will be the art of doing nothing at all.

Katharine Whitehorn, Observer column, 1970

There is a chilling moment in *The Stepford Wives*, Ira Levin's grim little fable of the consumer age (which was made into a film by Bryan Forbes) when one of the women realizes that her best friend has been replaced by a perfect imitation – a mechanical doll. She knows what has happened because, in the supermarket, instead of throwing the goods into the cart at random, the 'creature' stacks them up in a precise, ordered fashion just as the husbands think it should be done in the name of efficiency.

Perhaps real-life husbands who demand or dream of precision in all things, and in their wives in particular, are in some kind of telepathic contact with the creators of the robot-like women who still appear in 'kitchen' commercials on television and in other forms of advertising. (Different, sexier, or more glamorous robots appear in ads for cigars or drink or perfume.)

The advertising agencies, of course, would say that they pay more attention to the manufacturers' requirements, the product itself and to their own research into women, than to husbands. But it is clear that the image they have created has a bizarre life of its own that ever conscious efforts by some advertisers and outcry from many women has not been able to dispel.

The kitchen commercial woman has bright eyes and good

hair; she dresses casually but crisply. She smiles the timeless, ring-of-confidence smile showing her perfect teeth. Her hands, complete with wedding ring, may get roughed up by her labours but are soon smoothed away by changing to the right product. This charming android has so far ruled her kitchen unthreatened by the new working, thinking, arguing woman. She has a kind of mid-Atlantic quality about her which is scarcely surprising since we have tended to follow where the Americans have led both in consumerism and in advertising. It is however possible that the Americans are more devoted to this particular household goddess than we are in Britain. (One New York agency even has a lewd shorthand: 'TCK Commercials' – TCK for 'two cunts in a kitchen'.)

Rena Bartos, vice president and director of communications development for J. Walter Thompson in New York wrote not long ago: 'the target is woman: not fixed or stationary. It has moved 100 years in the last ten and it's accelerating. But many companies are still locked into the stereotyped woman of the 1950s. She does not any longer exist, perhaps never existed. But according to some advertising, the American woman has not changed her dress or her ideas for twenty-five years.'

Rena Bartos was able to point to some stereotypes still familiar in American advertising. British viewers will recognize them too. 'Honey Bunch', for instance: 'Do you know many women who hang in there breathless until Big Daddy gives her the definitive nod of her new brand of instant coffee, margarine or pantyhose? Do you know many men who give definitive nods?' 'Super Sweep' and the 'My-Shine-Beats-Your-Shine' woman are two others. You can imagine their behaviour. 'If you had no source of information but the advertising you'd seen,' Rena Bartos went on, 'you'd conclude that women almost never travel. And of course they never travel on business. An endless stream of business men streams in and out of airplanes, automobiles and hotels.' This is true in Britain too: travelling women are either the servants – stewardesses, desk clerks for rent-a-car trying harder all the time, or cosy grannies going to see their loved ones. The British Airways campaign for 1978/79 showed the same very pretty hostess 'taking more care of' two very different passengers. One was a man, with the voice-over of his

31

wife telling what happened the last time he went to New York on business. The man next to him (in a jumbo-load of sober suited dollar earners) got carried away by the William Tell overture on his earphones and the hostess plugged him into the 'Fly the flag' jingle for fun. The other showed a middle-aged woman on her way home from a holiday in Greece clutching a vase that every other single person on the flight has bought too. The implication was that she has never travelled beyond Bognor Regis before in her life.

Rena Bartos found few depictions of working women in American advertising, although, as in Britain, more than fifty per cent of adult women work outside the home. 'Once in a while a working woman is portrayed. She's a nurse (not a doctor), or a secretary, and she is on the hunt for male quarry. Or if married she is scurrying home from the office to take her housewifely tasks anxiously in hand.' Bartos does, however, report a mini-trend towards depicting the woman who is happily fulfilled in traditional areas – as a wife and mother – and who in addition holds a job she likes.

So 'What is a housewife these days?' she asked. 'Three out of five women are also working women. They work because they want the money, because they need it. A job is a passport to the outer world. Among full-time housewives, about half say that they plan to go back to work in the future – not fact, but a factor in their thinking.' Bartos warned of the problem of 'targeting' to the stay-at-home housewife, and the woman who works, and the one who plans to return some day. 'Was it the stay-at-home or the plan-to-work housewife who answered the doorbell when the interviewer came round? Was it the stay-at-home or the plan-to-work housewife who answered the phone for the day-after recall interview which determines the fate of so much advertising?'

She hinted that researchers may be relying too heavily on the most easily available women – that is those who are in the home during the day. Is this another reason why the old stereotype survives?

Does it partly explain why, back in Britain, such advertisements as a recent horror for Ajax scouring powder, still appear on our screens? That one showed two freshly ironed and coiffed women, standing in a kitchen gasping with almost orgasmic pleasure as they saw how clean the sink was after using the product. A big red bow sprang across the basin to seal the transformation, and a perfect TCK was complete.

Perhaps. But Patricia Mann of J. Walter Thompson in London could point to positive changes. First, she said, there has been much greater concentration on products rather than people in the past ten years. This applies particularly to food advertising, which now tends to exclude people from the film or picture altogether: 'I did a survey not long ago and looked at every food ad I could find to see how women were portrayed,' said Patricia Mann. 'They weren't; because there weren't any women in the ads. The script wasn't even saying "mums do it this way" or "working wives do it this way". It was left for whoever was the provider to take what he or she wanted out of it.'

There is also, she points out, much less of the 'slice of life' approach than there was even eight years ago, although there are some witty ones around, or miniature situation comedies. 'They do not ask people to identify with the characters, they simply ask to be noticed, it's saying we don't take ourselves too seriously.'

At the same time Patricia Mann said she thought there was more targeting directly to women, either as a specific group, or as a sub-group of campaigns: Guinness or the banks have done this. 'Three or four years ago we were looking at the whole range of people that could use banking services – and just one of those happened to be the independent woman with her Access card and her cheque card. Paint is another area. The DIY market is at last beginning to realize that women *do* paint, and put things together as well as men. It used to be always the guy who was up the ladder and the wife coming in to admire it or tell him that the tea was ready.'

But in terms of a woman's mothering, homemaking role, it was more difficult to identify the changes. That is partly, said Patricia Mann, because women live very complicated and various lives: 'For instance it is perfectly possible for someone like me to have a homemaking role, and a job role, and a want-to-feel-sexy role; there are all sorts of aspects of the same person. What has happened in response to this is that the image in ads

33

has become more ambiguous. The ambiguity is very, very important.'

It has also caused the people who seek to get their marketing strategy right a few headaches. 'There is some evidence to suggest that a career woman is a very acceptable image to the twenty to thirty age group – to talk to them about using deodorant soaps for instance. That fits in with being a production assistant in a studio, or a busy air stewardess meeting people all day. But if you show a very aggressive career woman who is highly competent and managing very very well, she may create resentment among the older women at home, who might say "what does she know about running a home. I'm the expert, I do it full time, she only does it part time". If you use ambiguity, you don't specifically turn on particular groups but you don't turn off others. You don't preach or threaten.' Which raises a crucial point in the matter of modern sales techniques: the soft sell. 'Hectoring advertisements are bad,' said Patricia Mann firmly. 'It's like being talked to by a hectoring salesman. You would rather buy from someone who takes some account of who you are, or who at least appears to be listening to you, and being reasonable. If the salesman is the type you can't shut the door on, well – there are advertisements like that, and they don't work. Television advertising is intrusive anyhow, but if an advertisement is gratuitously intrusive then I think it does the client (the manufacturer) more harm than good.'

The arrival of ambiguity, Patricia Mann declared, has signalled the exit of what she called the Archetypal Daz Mum. 'She was meant to be classless, but was actually slightly upper class; she had no accent or was Scottish because nobody thinks that a Scottish accent has class connotations. I think real people *are* presented these days. Oil of Ulay for instance, has three remarkably plain women talking about the benefits of the cream. I don't know what the results are but it must have a very high credibility score. They are not beauties, but are making the most of themselves and keeping themselves nice, which is a very strong motivation for some people. On the other hand it might turn some people off. They might say, God, I don't want to use that if it's used by bags like that. Anyway it is interesting that they have moved away from the glamorous model stereotype.'

By real, of course, Patricia Mann meant *realistic*. Real people are used in commercials but they tend to come over wooden and down beat. Patricia Mann cited the Hedex ad which had Mums standing outside a school talking about why they took Hedex to cure headaches. 'It doesn't work because real people are boring and stilted and they aren't used to being filmed. They are intrusive in a different kind of way. Two other dreadful ads were for night storage heaters and Avon cosmetics. The automatic response from me is that Avon makes your ears stick out, because the woman comes in absolutely wagging. Storage heaters make your teeth stick out because all the people in that are goofy. The more distracted you are by things like the ears and the teeth and the flat voices, the more you are not listening to the message. People say they think you should use real people but then they say, not real people like that. What they want is a slightly glamorized version of themselves. The great advantage of stereotypes is that they create a situation without subtracting from the message.'

The message is, of course, 'buy my wares'. But perhaps the 'real' people problem could be solved if the real people chosen were not stuck in front of the cameras like stuffed ducks and made to speak an idiot script – usually in the form of answering questions from an elderly disc-jockey type *man* (Crowther, Freeman, Wogan and their ilk.) Dandruff shampoos are sold in this way, so are soap powders and margarine. They seem to *aim* for a stilted effect. On the other hand dog food ads have 'real' breeders endorsing the product and clearly a hell of a lot of work has gone into making them at least keep up with the performance given by the dogs. Freddie Laker got a great deal out of the real people he was filmed greeting as they came off Skytrain in New York. There was the great bonus of the woman who rushed and flung her arms around him saying 'You're Wonderful'. All utterly authentic, as he explained: the American rules would not permit rehearsal or contrivance. But of course, as Patricia Mann was quick to say, with someone like Laker the image and the man become almost interchangeable.

The women's movement, in many guises, has attacked the use of the female image in advertising. But Patricia Mann saw their news and propaganda as only one, and not necessarily the most important, influence on what advertisers are doing and how they use women. 'I think that time all by itself is making a difference, because things cannot stand still. So is the continued, rather than the increased, use of research; when it is continuous you can monitor trends and changes. On individual advertisement research you can compare attitudes from different target groups and so on.

Look at the two Flash commercials which have been on and off the air from time to time. There is one which is a series with Molly Weir (the Scots comedienne), which is becoming increasingly remote from people who don't have chars any more. The second is about Mrs Black and Mrs White (*that* went to the race relations board). Mrs White used Flash, and got finished faster than Mrs Black and was able to get to school in time to fetch her kids. That again is terribly dated.

'Women are in general shown as being much more competent, whatever their role. There she is, she can't even get the floor washed and pick up the child from the school gates at a fixed time which everyone knows is fixed. And there's the poor little bugger waiting at the school gates. It comes over very badly because people are becoming overwhelmingly more independent and more competent in whatever they are doing and however they are doing it . . .'

Patricia Mann pointed with some wry amusement to a new and interesting character who had appeared in advertising in the last couple of years: the incompetent husband. He falls off ladders, he can't work the toaster in Anchor butter, he can't remember to buy the right cream crackers, he can't quite do anything. Alongside him is the New Supermum – here I borrow Patricia Mann's tag and call her the Daz Mum's daughter – who can apparently do *everything*: house, kids, food and still has time for the coffee break. Perhaps, hinted at in the background, she even works outside the home.

Then, Patricia Mann reminded, there is the Double Act: 'MacDougall's pudding mix, which has got a sauce on the bottom and a sponge on the top, shows the husband and wife making it together. The husband is being very pontifical and saying "the sauce always ends up on the top", and trying to have the last word. It's not quite the dumb blonde thing, it's much more overt

36

because it is a challenge of the sexes. They are both there to-gether doing it and it's great fun. The equivalent of that eight years ago might have been the Rise and Shine ad with the dumb blonde saying "it's like orange juice without any pips, how can you tell the difference?" The St Bruno tobacco dumb blonde, on the other hand, plays it for all it's worth and then comes up with a self-deprecating punch line, which is another interesting varia-tion. There are more husbands in ads generally, more humour attached to women, less clearly defined situations. Ads are be-ginning to say that women have got enough confidence to stand up and make a joke.'

The Equal Opportunities Commission, Patricia Mann believed, has made advertisers, particularly in the recruitment area where the Act is most specific, much more aware of what they are doing. 'But I don't think that the feminist movement has pro-duced any of the hard facts that people need to work on.' She felt that there had been a lot of emotive writing and talking about ads from a feminist viewpoint but no real understanding of how advertisements work or of what the women they were selling to wanted. Response to ads, she was sure, is not always rational. 'People see what they want to see, what they look for. If you are determined to see that the people in commercials are all incom-petent dumb blondes, or super efficient career women, or what-ever, then you will see very many more of those characters that you find objectionable than actually appear.' But of course it is the aim of advertising to persuade you that you have seen and heard something everywhere, so it is a kind of success when it works in reverse.

Advertising pundits tend to say that the social images they deploy are a fair reflection of society as it is and was. To be successful, they argue, an ad must follow a bit rather than lead. Patricia Mann repeated that it depended very much on your target groups: 'Middle class women who have always been housewives and stay-at-home get put off by aggressive career women. Young women, who are experimental and aspirational and looking to careers, not just doing something before they get married, who are much more advanced and liberated in lots of ways, can take fewer traditional stereotypes and images.

'The question that is always asked is "How much does she

37

know about what she is trying to sell me?''. Therefore, if you show somebody cooking you tend to choose somebody who knows about cooking. There is a New Zealander called Romain Blade who does ads for New Zealand lamb and she says "Here's a new way of treating it". It's never explicit whether she's a PRO for the NZ Lamb Board, or a housewife, or a New Zealander living in this country, or all three. I don't think it matters, and that is what I mean by ambiguous. She shows you how to carve a shoulder of lamb, which is riveting and interesting, because it is traditionally a male job. It isn't important in terms of whether she is a liberated working woman; it is important because she can show you how to do it and that she proves herself a know-ledgeable competent woman who produces a good result at the end. It would nevertheless have been difficult to do without establishing Romain Blade as some kind of meat expert, because if you had not it would have been distracting. If OXO-cube Katie had carved the meat ten years ago the image would not have sold OXO cubes. People would have been entirely distracted by the woman doing the carving.

'There is a Hoover ad which says "we'll liberate you" by get-ting you round the house more quickly. It is so overt that you want to say piss off to them. People don't want the word liber-ated thrown in their faces and they particularly don't want it used in connection with pushing a Hoover round the house quickly or otherwise. It's all right if you are selling a washing machine that is going to do all the washing while the woman is at work, or out of the house.

'In any ad, if the marketing is showing, it's a bad ad. House-wives that you talk to, ordinary working women, the people in the target group, are much more sophisticated and knowledge-able about how things work. They have seen on their televisions how commercials are made, they will criticize the lighting and the quality of the photography. One said to me when we had a group in to look at an ad "You are overdoing the country image".'

People, maintained Patricia Mann, are thinking much more for themselves; they are flattered when their opinions are asked. 'When they really know that they are being listened to, they will go into a lot of detail, and they really are very well informed, whether it is about other products in the same category, and why they have dismissed them for one reason or another, or whether it is about how they expect the product under discussion to be presented. You could never sell After Eight chocolates by showing a bloke giving them to his girlfriend in a transport cafe. Even if that happened in real life, it is just not what the product is all about. People buy it to give and it would debase it for them to show it like that.'

What a product is 'really about' is something in the joint, if not always matching, imaginations of the manufacturers and the advertisers. It may be easy for them to sit down and say now we are going to market a glamorous choc for people to eat after a smart dinner or for a man to give his girlfriend, and to play on the aspirations of people who would like to do these things. What happens when the same philosophy is applied to the kitchen and products which every woman can see have more to do with slavery than sophistication? However hard they listen – and I believed Patricia Mann when she said that the people who create ads do listen – to the samples of the 'target group', they only use the information so gathered as one factor in the creation of the finished image. They also listen to the manufacturer who is their client and who wants them to play safe, and use techniques and images that have worked before.

What comes out often enough is another version of the After Eight/Milk Tray marketing theory – that you can best sell consumer goods in terms of the buyers' aspirations, fantasies and self-image. Women, runs this line of thought, do not really want warts-and-all pictures of themselves wielding the scouring powder, instant dinner, or margarine that is going to change their domestic grind, or their husband's judgement of their cooking, or whatever. They want to see themselves translated to a Never-Never land where housework is not a demeaning burden, where cooking and child care are important and demanding but utterly within the competence of Supermum. Hence the stereotype that so irritates those who know in their heads and hearts it's not like that. Since everyone knows that advertising is there to sell, it perhaps shouldn't matter too much. But since it is, as Patricia Mann has said, so intrusive and indeed so all-pervasive, advertising does tend to feed into, and reinforce, old notions of what a housewife should be.

Patricia Mann felt that it was difficult to talk about social images in advertisements because you see much clearer reflections of them in the editorial content of magazines and television programmes, and on the news. 'You will never see a hint of the permissive society in an advertisement. If you show somebody with a child, she will wear a wedding ring on her finger. If you talk to people, they all say that the permissive society is here to stay because they have seen it on TV (they will probably say they have seen it in ads, but they haven't). They also have very firm ideas about what should be allowed to be shown in plays etc. and what should appear in commercials. Ads have to be much more moral, much more respectable: they have to avoid bad language and work by a code which is really ten years out of date. It is immensely offensive to break that code for commercial purpose. You will never see an ad for spirits on television. People stop after one pint; they sip their drinks and, above all, they always drink in company. You are always taking the most responsible route, the most proven route, the most universally acceptable route. It has to be tried and tested.

'I think it is important to realize that whatever kind of woman you put into an advertisement, whether it is a stereotype or a new look, how she is perceived depends entirely on the attitudes of people watching. If you think drinking is wrong you will see harmful images in a beer ad. You get lots of different responses to a new chocolate bar advertisement for instance. If it were being viewed by someone who loved chocolate, someone else who loved chocolate but knew that it gave her spots, and someone else who loved chocolate but was on a diet, you would get three different reactions. They are all in the market for chocolate but the attitudes are so different. The ones who like it but feel they shouldn't eat it are immensely resentful at you for bringing it into their living rooms.'

The 'success' of a particular advertising campaign is monitored and assessed in a number of ways and according to what the aim was in the first place. And of course advertising is in itself only one part of the entire marketing strategy: packaging, distribution, pricing and display are equally if not more important in the manufacturer's sales drive. All may work in combination so that a woman may in the end see a vision of herself in a nice clean kitchen with that red bow over the sink that has been cleaned with Ajax. Ugh, she might well think, who do they think they are kidding. But when she goes into Tesco or Safeway or her local supermarket, she may see a display of new Ajax and, because she has used it before, or because she needs a cleanser anyway and it is on special offer and because it is right there in her way, she may buy it. What she feels when she next sees the Ajax ad, or what she feels when she is cleaning the sink is another matter.

Patricia Mann emphasized that sales alone are no indication of whether an advertisement has been successful. 'You may find that because a new giant Safeway has opened they are offering Persil Automatic at a lower price, and it sells out in a week because women are buying six packets at once. But it is pretty rare that someone will spend £10 in a week on soap powder, but look what it does to the sales figures when it happens.

'There are certain areas in which you can tell immediately how effective an advertisement has been. Those are the classified ads where you pick up a phone and say you want to sell a second hand pram. You can actually say, "That cost me £4. I have had twenty-five replies and I sold it to the second man who called." You can say that it worked. If you are selling products exclusively for mail order you can make some intelligent guess about how it's working. But if you are trying to make comparisons between whether someone has seen an ad, or shopped around and found the product best, you can't separate the two.

'All women say they ignore ads, that they are never affected by them and yet they are the ones who say "well, actually I have tried x, y and z", when x and y aren't actually in the shops yet, they are just being advertised. It is all part of a sieving process. We could never be aware of noticing all the things we notice every day. It is the familiar or the relevant, or something that tells you it's for you, that gets through to you. Women who shop around build up a reservoir of information which they store in their sub-conscious and dip into it when they need it.'

And of course advertisers eagerly dip into and feed into this subconscious to the best of their ability.

Nevertheless Patricia Mann was sure that the stereotype of the housewife they use to do this is less stereotyped than it was. 'It is fluffier round the edges, more open to individual interpretation.' She also believed that the image we retain of what is on the screen is very out of sync with what is actually there. Thus viewers will cite campaigns which have been off the air for years. But yes, she admitted, there were still quite a lot of women shown serving food, standing round the table while the others eat, joining in last. 'But this,' she said, 'is surely not an untrue reflection of what goes on. If you had the husband standing round serving, people would be distracted by the image. Women would say "that woman is so bossy and henpecking that she gets her husband to wait at table". It just wouldn't work.' She did not pose another alternative to this crude reversal, although some advertisements have shown couples working together in the kitchen, and a bloke making his girl a cup of tea.

Patricia Mann did not reckon that advertising was usually sufficiently avant-garde to be inspirational or have much influence on how people lived their lives. 'An example from years ago, when Flash was first introduced – the marvellous new product that cleaned floors without producing lather. It was shown with women using a sponge mop. What that did as a commercial was sell more sponge mops than Addis could make. People pick up ideas from ads. They select those that are appropriate to them and reject those that aren't. But people don't go around copying the kitchens or the living rooms they see in ads. If you showed a woman in a really grotty kitchen washing the floor with Flash, it would come over as a grotty product in a way. If you show her in a reasonably nice kitchen, it doesn't get in the way. If you show her in an ultra modern kitchen, then it ought to be reflecting an ultra modern aspect of the produce and she might think that's the way she should be.

'If you are about to make a change in your life – a new cooker, fridge, curtains etc. – then you'll pick up ideas but you won't take what you see in commercials as a blueprint. There are so many alternatives, an enormous range of lifestyles from which you can make a conscious choice.

'For instance, one of the things you can *always* buy cut price is an Echo hostess trolley. If you take the number of times you see it advertised as an indication of how many people buy them, you would think everyone had one or that everyone is rushing round entertaining and needing one. I don't think anyone would think in those terms. They might think it was a nice thing to have but mightn't quite know what to do with it or where to put it or they'd think, "God, I bet it would go wrong for me".

'On the other hand there has never to my knowledge been an advertisement for an illuminated cocktail cabinet. But if you go to a council estate it is amazing how, if one household has acquired one, others soon follow suit. That kind of example is very important. It's local, it's near you, and people can come in and see what you've got and what you've not got. It's what people have, rather than what's being shown to everybody. And the more you can't find the money to buy all the things you are shown the more you pick out the things that are relevant to you.'

In the end, said Patricia Mann, 'it is the product that creates and dictates the role you show the woman in. If you are showing a cooker, or a floor cleaner or a vacuum, it would be a distraction to show a man. But if you show a woman, she could illustrate any aspect of the housewife, who just happens to be in charge of getting things done. So that's why you saw it like it is.'

Showing it like it is is an advertising credo: 'Are you fair, honest, legal, decent and truthful? Advertisements have to be' is the self-advertisement of the Advertising Standards Authority, the body which acts as an arbiter of standards. It aims to keep advertising within the law and accepted standards of morality, and away from the manipulative practices of which advertising is often (fairly and unfairly) accused. The ASA decides on how much of a female body the public eye can take without blinking. It weighs the dangers involved in too much or the wrong kind of advertising of commodities, such as alcohol and tobacco, and it has a number of rules about children. It is very concerned with tastes, with acceptable images, but is not over concerned with the female *image*. 'This advertisement degrades women' was the famous feminist slogan of the sixties which got slapped over ads for undies on the tube. Neither the ASA nor the advertisers are too worried about such protests unless the standards of the majority of people who see the advertisement are also degraded or outraged. 'We have had no complaints' a man at the ASA told Polly Toynbee of the *Guardian* when she asked him why the Authority had taken no action over sexist images.

Let us leave aside the Lamb's Rum girl, striding rubber clad either in or out of the sea, which is a piece of male fantasy and not an erosion of women's daily picture of themselves, and consider the housewife who has had a terrible day. Burst pipes, plumbers, rampant kids and all manner of disasters have beset her. She blurts it all out as she helps hubby off with his coat in the evening. But the ad turns out to be for a particularly comfortable kind of armchair 'for every man who's wife has had a hard day'. As he sinks back oblivious, the fraught lady melts, smiles indulgently and produces a cup of tea. A neat joke of course, and harmless enough. But it is also a play on the widely accepted notion that only men have hard days, possibly in jungles or the outposts of the empire, but usually at the office frontier. As Ann Oakley pointed out, women's work is nonwork and therefore enjoys non status.

The notion is that domestic service by the housewife should be a form of grateful servitude to the man who is, after all, shouldering all the burdens that really matter and of course bringing home the bulk of the cash to pay for the plumber and the comfortable chair. The more a man earns, the less a woman *needs* to contribute to the coffers, the higher the income or class group the couple achieve, the more diminished the woman seems. She becomes a status symbol in herself and her daily grind must hide behind a gleaming array of labour-saving gadgets. The more gleaming and arrayed her kitchen, the less seriously we can take her complaints about having a hard day. It is a vicious circle.

Working class women are not often portrayed in ads except in miniature situation comedies or public safety films. But the 'ordinary' Mrs Average housewife is given a little more dignitas than her up-market sister. All advertisements trade on aspirations. But in the household goods and chattels area they come close enough to reality to be dangerous. While success-fully selling their product, they may also be selling an image, a set of standards that may not be relevant to a particular woman but may make her feel that somehow she is a failure or *below* standard. That there is a housewifely norm is a comforting illusion, but it is an illusion. The 'ambiguous woman' is a start towards dispelling it, but is not enough. Too often she is not only ambiguous but mechanical, bland, too perfect – the new stereo-type, if you like, of the Supermum who can do everything, even make herself look good in T-shirt and jeans.

But is the bland assumption that whatever a woman may be doing besides her housework and child care, those last are res-ponsibilities on which she will never relax her grip and which will never relax their grip upon her? The idea seems to be that of course women can have careers/jobs/outside interests that could be useful/therapeutic/interesting for her, but only pro-vided she can fulfil her first duty to hearth and home and hus-band properly first. Being a Supermum, or thinking that she ought to be, puts an immeasurable strain on women. It is unfair on those who do seek to combine many roles because it shows them an image difficult if not impossible to attain; and it is equally unfair on the woman who is still in the throes of early child care and total domesticity.

It is not of course the fault of advertising agencies or their clients that women are in a difficult and transitional period of history. They are, after all, there to sell products, many of which will help women in one way or another in a practical sense. But I believe that because they are in such a powerful position, be-cause of the money they are able to spend on consumer research, because they know so much about women, these people could be helpful in another way. The notion that only a bland image sells has no doubt been proven, but the success of different kinds of ads shows that it is not the only way. Food advertising which shows only the product is one example. But when people are shown – and ads would be boring if there were never any human beings in them – greater use of individual image, more revela-tion of what women actually do, would surely be possible. Somewhere between shoving a mike under the nose of a nervous and flat-voiced 'real' woman who says that yes definitely, she prefers Vosene, or Stork, or Daz, and the composite ambiguous Supermum there must be a million versions of women's life which the subtlety and skill of advertising could project.

I believe that people buy products because they need them or are attracted to them in some way; surely there is no reason to believe that they would be put off by seeing the product endorsed not by a fantasy woman intended to embrace as many aspects of the contemporary woman as possible, but by a woman who has at least one of the problems that women share today and at least one of the great new advantages. I am not proposing to do the agencies' work for them – nor could I; simply to suggest that some of them (and there are some splendid ads) try a little harder to use the expensive and valuable information they are constantly in the business of collecting. Some of the very best directors and actors are now often employed to produce a television commercial. All that is missing is the script.

Dizzy Hens and the New Dialectic

... the washing machine and the cleaner seem to be starting the change of life. The cleaner in particular refuses to pick up anything. Hardly a day passes without the driving band cutting its throat on a bit of shredded bone (the puppy again) and I always seem to rupture those cleaner bags. You force them on like condoms and end up in a cloud of dust.

Jilly Cooper, Housework, 1975
(column in the *Sunday Times*)

Mothers have the really horrible job of teaching their daughters to be second class citizens. That's where we think a woman learns to act against herself, or rather, learns unwittingly to co-operate in her own subordination.

Cathy Haw and Rosie Parker, *Spare Rib*, No. 61

Almost exactly ten years ago, in November 1970, Mary Stott, OBE, the doyenne of modern women's page editors, asked the readers of Woman's Guardian a rough question: 'Are you a slave or a slut?' she enquired. If a market researcher turned up on their doorsteps and asked a lot of questions of the 'how often do you clean the oven/windows/bath' variety, would they give honest answers? If not why not? Did they prefer to order their housework by hygiene or common sense or appearance? Did they keep a daily schedule?

She then reminded them that, ten years before that, in 1960, the Institute of House Workers (where are they now?) had revised their Simple Guide to Housework, giving daily and weekly schedules for all the housecleaning jobs. Mary Stott quoted their suggested schedule for the 'daily clean of the starcase and hall'. It read like instruction for some kind of religious observance:

47

'Sweep outside the front door and porch.

Close front and room doors.

Brush stairs lightly using a small hard brush and dustpan for the carpet, and a small soft brush for the paint surround. Work from the top downwards.

Mop linoleum and polished wood floor and surrounds'.

The guide continued to work downwards in this fashion until the dusting of banisters, furniture and any ledges was complete. Daily work in sitting rooms and all other rooms was also specified.

Mary Stott wondered if her readers found this 'funny, pathetic or, even though only ten years old, just totally out of date'. She went on to prod her audience into thinking about their attitudes to their own domestic chores. Did they like housework or loathe it? Did the equation of the creation of a nice home, in return for their husband's financial support and gratitude seem a balanced one? She then asked them to consider a reader's letter she had received from a woman in her late fifties.

Denying that she was 'self martyring and masochistic', the woman declared that she had been all her active life 'obliged, not by my husband, not by my children, but by the set-up of the male dominated society into which I have been born enslaved, because I am female, to be a domestic servant to my family. This goes for the vast majority of women, old or young, married or single, money-making or not and whether they like it or detest it.' This woman wasn't interested even in family participation to lighten the load. 'I don't want to do the bloody jobs at all, with or without help.'

Mary Stott's 'questionnaire' and most of the many letters that answered it, had an ironic, gently self-mocking tone which was typical of the thinking women's journalism of the sixties. For the first time women were questioning their scouring role and the restrictions involved in performing it. Strangely enough it was housework and not child care that was seen as the main bar to freedom: slavery lurked with the dust under the bed or behind the cupboards, not in the cradle. No longer could a woman, who was probably at least as well educated as her husband, see the sweeping of a room or the burnishing of a kettle as part of a high calling. Nor with the aid of the new machines was it quite drudgery. What was it exactly and why was *she* doing it?

Mary Stott, whose page in the *Guardian* not only stirred its readers to thought but to action (organizations such as The National Housewives Register, the Pre-School Playgroups Association and many others sprang from articles and letters she printed) was not the first to cotton onto the 'slave or slut' theme. In December 1963 (the year *The Feminine Mystique* was published in America) Katharine Whitehorn wrote one of the seminal pieces of 'women's' journalism this century. People who don't buy the *Observer* and who cannot remember another word that the Whitehorn column has ever contained, recall what she had to say about sluts and sluttery. 'It changed my life', I have been told more than once by a contemporary.

'This article,' wrote Whitehorn (who had recently given up being the *Observer*'s fashion editor) 'is dedicated to all those who have ever changed their stockings in a taxi, brushed their hair with somebody else's nail brush or safety pinned a hem.' Ask yourself, she suggested, whether you have ever 'taken anything back out of the dirty clothes basket because it had become relatively the cleaner thing?' Apart from being hilariously funny, the column touched the guilty nerve of all those middle class women who have, as I have already pointed out, had to face life in the second half of this century without servants whether paid (maids and nannies) or unpaid (aunts, grannies, unmarried daughters or cousins). They had been trying to keep up a perfect home front, cook wonderfully, strip the pine, do the upholstery, bring up the children, and probably do some kind of other job (or aspire to do so) as well.

It was an impossible task. Once they shoved a finger into one hole in the dyke, a leak was bound to spurt somewhere else. So Whitehorn's witty designation of the race of sluts was an amazing relief. Everything was all right; and from then on that scatty, throw-away rolling-the-eyes-while fishing the knickers out of the salad bowl approach was one way of putting a brave face on a pretty raw deal. It was also a way of saying (remember *The Stepford Wives*) 'I'm a person, not some kind of mechanical doll that does the housework.' As we all know, the right to identity was one of the first cries of the feminist movement.

It is possible to trace two strains in 'women's' journalism back to Whitehorn's sluts : the first could be seen in the whole school of her imitators, and in certain semi-glossy magazines which sprang up to pour a gushy veneer over the dreaded transition to middle age that marriage and children brings. 'Ugh, forty year old women, trying to be the girls,' said one scornful colleague about *Over 21* magazine in its early days, and the style which I call dizzy hen, or early Superwoman. Shirley Conran has taken things a stage further, and made her fortune writing books in that tone of voice – hard facts and valuable information all dressed up in nonchalance, inverted proverbs and fake scattiness. In America, someone told her she had founded a religion; but I and many others feel that 'Superwoman' is one of the saddest, and ironic and dangerous labels women have ever been daubed with, as we move towards some semblance of equality and liberation.

The dizzy hens from whose eggs Shirley's superwoman hatched gushed, used rude words at funny-outrageous moments, talked about their 'boyfriends' when they were at least forty, and giggled over 'intercourse cigarettes' and other Upper Fourth type jokes. They played down their education, their problems, and even the money which their husbands often earned in large quantities. But, even in cases where they did jobs themselves they seemed to feel the need to retain a spurious femininity by indulging in self deprecation and a Shirley MacLaine kind of lovable zaniness.

They took to the new style in clothes like ducks to a pond; dungarees and tee-shirts and casual chic all but abolished middle age for them. Matronliness was out. 'What did we all do before there was knitted cotton' I heard one smartish lady exclaim at a party sometime around 1973. And it really was true, not just a magazine con trick. Look at the photograph album of any woman who is now in her late thirties and forties. The snaps of her in her teens will almost certainly present a *more* middle-aged, got-up sort of image than the *plein air* grown up girl she has become : trim, corsetless, and far more subtle in the use of make up than her mother, or herself when young, could ever have been. There was no concession here to the feminist no-make-up-no-artifice ethic. Casual chic required and requires, great skill, and quite a lot of money; these women were as keen to make themselves beautiful for their husbands or lovers as any nineteenth century coquette. They were not brash and predatory like the *Cosmopolitan* cover girl, nor sweet and homely like the *Woman* woman; who knows there might lurk a matriarch, or an icemaiden or a helpless frightened woman under their ingenue look and girlish deep-cleansed skin. The trick was not to let it show; to keep a stiff lower chin. It required a ruthless determination to do so and any who managed it would indeed be Super-women, confections of pure steel with marzipan frosting.

In another direction, the horizons that Katharine Whitehorn herself scanned were much wider. She was the first of the new 'clever' women of Fleet Street : undeniably female, but with the wit and stomach of a man. At least that is how male readers and editors saw it. She started her career on the *Spectator* and *Picture Post*, before being temporarily drawn into the harem of women's magazines and fashion writing. But she had the gift of relating the most harem-bound subjects to the outside world, of making anything she wrote about seem a subject of general interest.

Kinder, kirche und *kuche* may have been part of Whitehorn's material, but her irreverence about them and her ironic and aphoristic writing about men themselves was revolutionary : 'In one social bracket the man is the fixer because woman doesn't know how; in another all the fixing is done by the girl secret-aries to leave the tycoon free. Which is the position of power ?', she wrote in 1970.

Katharine Whitehorn joined *Woman's Own* in 1958. Before she was fired, or hoofed as she delicately puts it, eighteen months later, she learned one or two things she thinks the girls at *Spare Rib* would do well to know. The main one was just how upset people can stand to be made – about the world in general, but about themselves in particular. She also learned about reassuring readers which, in those days took a curious form. The formula on the advice pages was always that, if your husband had gone off you, it must be because *you* were coming down to breakfast in your curlers; it must be *your* fault. That, she notes with satis-faction, has changed totally.

Whitehorn has taken some trouble to analyse why her 'slut' piece caused such a stir. It was, she reckons, because before that any advice given to women was telling them to be perfect. Suddenly she among others was saying, it's not like that really, let's come dirty about it. However, she adds, it was all done in the manner of lighthearted attack, rather like schoolgirls – you don't believe that the whole building will crash around your ears if you prod it. The last decade has, she thinks, changed the things women, and her readers generally, are shocked by. When *That Was The Week That Was* started in the sixties, it seemed very daring to make jokes about religion and the Royal Family. When she wrote a piece in the early sixties saying that it was rotten that birth control was never discussed in the women's mags because of the Irish editions, the whole idea was shocking. Nowadays there are well organized pro and anti abortion lobbies; then there was just a vast national shocked reaction when the subject was mentioned.

Whitehorn is never quite sure whether a change in her readers' attitudes simply indicates that they are growing older along with her or whether there is a general shift, but ten years ago being steadily married seemed to be the norm; now it seems the beleaguered minority. But nowadays she reckons that women working when they have young children get less flack than she did for doing the same thing.

What Mary Stott was doing at the *Guardian* for the 'serious' side of women's journalism, Katharine Whitehorn thinks George Seddon and herself were doing more jokily and stylishly with the *Observer*'s EGO pages in the late sixties. 'We were tearing up the lace doyley. It was tremendous fun.'

It was also a huge revelation to Fleet Street (Jane Austen had clearly lived in vain) that any woman could be *funny*. Since the early sixties there have been a cavalcade of 'amusing' women journalists but none has reached Whitehorn's level either of fame or fun. Too often women columnists have followed instead the Glenda Slag pattern established by Jean Rook in the Daily Sketch, the Daily Mail and the Daily Express. Her brash, frank, Come-off-it-Princess-Anne, Who-do-you-think-you-are-Muhammed-Ali style is pretty awful.

But while groaning, it is well to remember that until the early sixties a woman in journalism, where she surfaced at all, did so at home hints level, or – a rare bird indeed – as a war or foreign correspondent, some kind of lonely exotic expert proving the rule. Women's pages, when they started to appear in the nineteenth century were essentially middle and upper class *housewives'* pages. They were cosy corners set aside for articles about etiquette, fashion, cookery and perhaps some uncontroversial medical advice, all much in the manner of the magazines already flourishing. The idea was to lure advertisers who, ironically, (as Judie Lannon pointed out) were offering more helpful information and instruction to women running a home than were editors. Editorial for women was all pretty anodyne. On the other hand when women appeared out of purdah on the news pages it was usually by contrast pretty disgraceful stuff. They were murderesses, or murder victims, prostitutes or runaway heiresses. Then, suddenly, worst of all, they were suffragettes.

I have not the space, nor the historical authority to examine why it was that after the trauma of the suffragette movement and two wars, two generations of men and women whose lives had gone through every kind of hoop, that the cosy cornerish, fireside atmosphere of women's pages endured right into the sixties and still has some expression today. If you ask a man (or many women) what a woman's page is likely to contain, the answer is usually a derisive 'oh, fashions and babies and how to make jam.' An aura of domesticity still hangs over the phrase, and of course, to the patriarch, domesticity is trivia. So, even the frank revelations of how women really think and feel, even accounts of the struggle for a place in employment and equality in the world at large take on some of the 'trivial' stigma.

At the *Guardian* where I worked for five years and which prides itself on both the space it has given to women writers and issues, and the jobs women journalists have achieved on its staff, the quite civilized men I worked with could scarcely mention a woman correspondent's or reporter's name (whatever her speciality) without using the word 'neurotic' or 'hysterical'. Male colleagues who indulged in far more prima donna-ish behaviour were, by contrast, fondly indulged.

Nevertheless the change *has* been dramatic. What happened? As late as 196? Jill Tweedie, who became the *Guardian*'s most famous columnist, was sitting in the women's page room at the *Sunday Telegraph* where she then worked. She loved it there, she says: it was carpeted wall to wall and coffee was brought to the desk and it felt very *safe*. It was like a womb. Then one day the women's editor, Winefride Jackson, appeared looking anxious. 'Listen to this girls,' she said . . . 'what do you think it means? Yoko Ono says here that women are the niggers of the world. What can she mean?' Mutters of puzzlement broke out all round her, but Jill says she can remember the thud of recognition in her own chest. She *did* know what it meant. Soon after that she emerged from the womb and moved to the *Guardian*.

There she found herself once a week filling a huge, advertisementless page, with about 4000 words a time. She was soon writing about the unwriteable: menstruation, death, abortion, childbirth, breast feeding, but from the women's *real* point of view – not in a patronizing quasi-mystical mother-knows-best style. All the subjects she wrenched out from behind the doctor's consulting room curtain and from under the cushions on the sofa at home are now so familiar as part of the guts and ovaries school of women's journalism that it is hard to believe they haven't been everyone's breakfast time conversation for a hundred years. So much so that groans greet any mention of the main themes: 'Oh no, not *that* again.'

But it should not be forgotten that things not taught in schools, nor discussed in very many homes were suddenly being set in type and, a bit later, debated on television and radio. Would the phone-in radio shows which deal with sexual and medical problems in the raw have been possible without people such as Jill Tweedie? I doubt it.

Women's feelings were being talked about as if they were a serious matter, and instead of being offered guides to good behaviour and to their own kitchens women readers were being offered what they were really asking for: guides to their own insides, both spiritual and gynaecological. They were also recognized as customers of the newspaper for the first time. The fact that a reader could report seeing on a commuter train in the mid sixties a perfectly respectable-looking man open his *Guardian* at Jill Tweedie's page, place it on the floor and jump up and down on it in fury, is a nice little illustration of how she touched certain nerves. Tweedie was not in any way a preacher or a missionary; she was an explorer and an enthusiast, and has done as much and more to popularize the tenets of feminism than any hardline campaigner.

The fact that the *Guardian* should have been, in the seventies, a touch schizophrenic (or should I say neurotic) about its famous women's page is really no more than a reflection of women's affairs. Are women separate, or should they be considered separately from men? Is it ghetto journalism? Is there a sub-division between women at home and women at work? Shouldn't women's subjects compete with others? They dropped the 'Woman's' label once for 'Miscellany' but returned to 'Guardian Women'. The debate continues. If men and women are equal, why not a men's page? If women are part of the world, why a separate page of their own? The increasing complexity of women's lives and the mixing of roles makes this confusion inevitable for a while longer.

To begin with it was simpler: the early success of Mary Stott was with women at home – housewives who were well educated and were using their degrees and diplomas to soak nappies and scrub floors. The 'captive wives' of that generation were also the activists of the Guardian Women's page which offered the other side of the dizzy hen's coin that may have been duller and worthier, but was genuinely about the search by women for a proper place in society – in relation to their men and their children and everything else. The problem, however, remains – what do you *do* with women's consciousness once you have raised it? Not everyone has an easily definable problem; not everyone can form a pressure group.

Further down market, the pop papers, in spite of the daily deference they pay to their ritual sex object on Page Three (a feature which seems to have become a tabloid talisman) have not had very adventurous women's pages until recently. The *Daily Mirror*, which of course has had Marje Proops answering problems for more than twenty years and running her column since the late sixties, has broadened its range of women's features and is tackling all the 'difficult' subjects with a new vigour. The *Sun* has the earthy and motherly Claire Rayner. But in spite of trail blazing in newspapers it is undoubtedly magazines that women turn to most for advice and entertainment.

The mass circulation weekly magazines, which have never

made any bones about the fact that their target is the housewife and mother, have, especially in the past five years, taken up the 'new' themes surrounding equality and liberation, and been discussing previously taboo subjects about which newspapers still tend to the prudish. Not so long ago, the editor of the *Observer* (on the face of things no prude) summoned me to express misgivings about a picture I had published without consulting him. It had showed a heavily pregnant woman, naked, with a man sitting next to her. It was a discreet, almost romantic picture: the image was of two people contemplating the birth of their wanted child. My editor was worried that it might have offended some readers. I hadn't shown it to him because this thought had not occurred to me – as it would have done for instance in the case of a sex-object pin-up. 'You must remember,' he rebuked me, 'that you women are very used to seeing this sort of thing in magazines and so on.' So whose *pudeur* was he worried about? Children, with pretty free access to the same magazines (no longer is the National Geographic the main source of human biology education) as well as to their mothers in various states of undress and gestation, might snigger at a certain age, or be curious at another. But *offended*? It all boiled down to the fact that it was male middle-aged squeamishness that was at risk.

Such a debate would not, in 1979, have taken place in any but the staidest magazine office. And although it has to be pointed out that the staidest of them *Woman's Weekly* 'famous for its knitting' is also the most successful, with a (1979) circulation of close to three quarters of a million, most journals have taken on the job of informing their readers about themselves and the world with a will. They will quite freely and graphically discuss sexual and gynaecological problems and tackle controversial moral and social questions, including homosexuality, abortion and AID with complete frankness.

Strangely, all this enlightenment has not altered the basic package that attracts housewives to the news-stands. *Spare Rib* with its downbeat stongly 'real' cover women may be making headway, with a circulation of more than 20,000 and a 'readership of six times that', but in its aim of reaching 'all women' it lags far behind its traditional rivals.

Spare Rib's presentation is deliberately unglossy and the

magazine makes a very direct approach to readers, inviting them to contribute ideas and articles and offering them a voice and participating role as far as possible. This policy may be a fair one, but it doesn't make for the sharpest copy. However, they are also not afraid to print critical letters. One reader in the issue of December 1978 wrote that, although she still loved the magazine, she felt it had changed and had become too identified with a feminist stereotype. 'I now feel an outsider because I am not slim/full time into feminism/active on marches/a Londoner/somebody's lover . . . I get the feeling that the magazine is getting more introspective and cliquey.'

In the same issue, however, another reader wrote to say how much she needed *Spare Rib* now that she had moved outside London. 'I have always been a little nervous of the real hardliners in the movement because they tend to be impatient, even unintentionally arrogant, with the doubting, the half hearted, the uncertain. For all those who march unerringly into the promised land aren't there just as many who could stumble in there by accident if given a hand?'

Part of *Spare Rib*'s trouble when it comes to mass readership appeal is, of course, that it concentrates uncomfortably on the starker realities of women's lives, constantly reminding them about discrimination, male domination and their vulnerability generally. Other magazines are escapist, drawing a veil over the less pleasant facts of life or, at least, presenting them in an upbeat breezy kind of way – sandwiched between the slimmer's guide and the romantic serial.

Woman, *Woman's Own*, *Good Housekeeping* and *Woman's Realm* and the rest still carry the same bright, pretty but not over-glamorized cover girl (varied occasionally with male tennis players, movie stars and royals); there is still lots of knitting and recipes and advice about make up and slimming. Many people, including my fellow journalist Lyn Owen, believe that the slightly sugary, prettified image of women that these magazines project owes too much to the advertising that buoys it up – and to the men who still own the companies that run the magazines. Obviously some of the editorial *is* there to catch advertising, but much of it is genuinely relevant to the women who buy the magazines. Housewives *do* cook, they *do* have children, and it *is* cheaper to knit and dressmake than to buy off the peg. What-ever the radical feminist line may say about make up and cos-metic self decoration, most women, especially young ones, enjoy dressing up and putting a bright face to the world. But whether they buy *Woman's Own* because they identify with the cover-girl or want to know more about the latest theory of child-raising or dangers of alcohol, is hard to determine. I am sure surveys could be conducted to prove either point.

But if the magazines sell too hard and make women feel (as they certainly did in the pre slut fifties) that they should be aspiring to an impossible level of perfect womanhood and ideal beauty, their influence does become pernicious. Few magazines in Britain could be accused of that now, although they are still to some extent guilty of an over-cosy protective attitude to their readers.

As Ruth Wallsgrove of the *Spare Rib* collective said, when that magazine opened in 1973 they hoped that it would to some extent counter the kind of fantasy promulgated by magazines such as *Woman* and *Woman's Own*. 'It wasn't just fantasy, it was such *narrow* fantasy they were offering then. But they have changed a lot.'

While preparing this chapter I looked closely at the current issues of two of these two top magazines, *Woman*'s circulation was 1,583,190; *Woman's Own*'s 1,578,234 – both a far cry from their days in the late fifties and early sixties when they hovered around the three million mark. The readership of the two maga-zines, however, adds up to nearly twelve million. In the last year or two both have earned praise for their reflections on the new concerns of women and for the surveys they have con-ducted into women's attitudes to marriage, men and themselves. These surveys are, to some extent, similar to those conducted by advertising agencies, the main difference being that they are made available to women, and get quoted on the BBC news. For example a *Woman* survey on marriage in 1978 found that women in the sixteen to twenty-four age group, were the most cynical about marriage; the majority would live with the same man again, but not marry him. Women over the age of forty were the most admiring of their husbands, while those under twenty-five tended to rate their husbands as 'average' or 'below average'.

An earlier survey by *Woman's Own*, which launched a campaign for a better pre-school child care facilities for women who work, found that four out of five women would want to work outside the home, even if there was no financial necessity. The *Woman* findings on the other hand claimed that seventy per cent of women who work outside the home only do so because of the money.

There were no surveys being unfolded in the week ending June 30, 1979. Indeed a quick glance could have fooled the reader into thinking that little had changed since 1956. With the exception of one article on *anorexia nervosa* (*Woman's Own*) with photographs showing how the young woman who died of it declined from robust health into haggard thinness (there was no slimming advice that week), the reading matter was fairly anodyne and relaxing. The problem pages however were sprinkled with letters about masturbation and spanking fantasies, which would probably not have been there ten or fifteen years ago. (Katharine Whitehorn recalls how, when she was at *Woman's Own*, the problem page always had a space at the end where they printed the answer and not the letter – 'Anxious, Basingstoke: Please don't worry, what you are doing is perfectly normal ...' etc. – the staff all used to run to the letters file to find out *what* it was the reader was doing ...)

Last June 30, *Woman* had a cover story on Prince Charles, Super Prince. There was an interview with Kenny Everett's wife (wives of the famous, particularly housewives of the famous have always been a good staple), a heartwarming story of how a handicapped boy gave his bone marrow to save his sister's life, and a run down on the Bond Girls past and present, to mark the launch of the new Bond movie, *Moonraker*. Plus of course all the usual magazine fare – horoscopes, make-up, diet and knitting. There were, however, some dropped stitches here and there to spoil the perfect pattern. In the serial, for example, which is a time-honoured part of the weekly magazine formula. This one, called 'The House Next Door', looked traditional enough, illustrated with a drawing of a haunted looking woman at a gloomy window. But the 'story so far' revealed a plot unthinkable ten years ago: 'Pie's father entered the guest room to find Buddy and his boss Lucas Abbott in a naked embrace. The shock proved fatal to the old man. Pie's screams brought Walter, myself and all the other guests running to witness the terrible scene.'

Whole packs of characters have been running to witness tableaux of this kind ever since romantic fiction was conceived on the hurly burly of some Regency chaise longue or other. But the embraces, have tended to the heterosexual and the unexplicit. Was this a breakthrough? Were the editors of *Woman* seeking by some subtle means to tell their readers more about homosexuality and what it means? Or was it just that melodrama needs a taboo ingredient to make it work, and ordinary boring old infidelity and sexual intercourse have lost their black magic? Later in the narrative all bets were covered by one character explaining to another, as to a child, that 'some of the most unlikely people in the world turn out to be homosexual, it's not all that unusual, tragic as it turned out for them (Buddy and Lucas). It was just horrible, but at least you can sort of understand.'

Woman's 'agony' page, once the repository of Evelyn Home's (Peggy Makins) careful, compassionate wisdom, was temporarily passed on to that most direct of advisers, Anna Raeburn. But even she, with her *Forum* training and lack of inhibition, seemed to assume an unwontedly staid tone for a while. Now the page is run by Virginia Ironside, and last June 30 she had an interesting assortment of letters. One was an ancient *cri de coeur* 'Do the wives of today know how to keep a husband or a happy home? Is their house a welcoming place or a railway station?' After much reminiscence about her grandmother's bottomless teapot and blazing fires, the reader wondered why more modern women didn't understand that 'If it's a cosy home, a husband never leaves, just says: "I would marry you, but my wife makes such a wonderful steak and kidney pudding that I can't." ' Ironside reminded her gently that comfort is not all material and cosiness is impossible if there is no happiness. 'What about the wife,' she wrote, who says "I would marry you, but my husband brings me such a delicious cup of tea in the morning that I can't." '

Immediately below this were two letters, one from a woman who had just discovered that her husband had a baby by another woman, and one who wondered how she could tell her husband of her spanking fantasies. 'If he's forty-seven and experienced, he won't find any request like yours strange,' was the reply. 'That doesn't mean he'll necessarily be keen to try it. But it's definitely worth asking him.'

In the same week, *Woman's Own* also had a feature on the Bond girls, the serial was *Oliver's Story* (son of *Love Story*). There was a profile of John McEnroe, 'Wimbledon's super new tennis machine', the anorexia story, and an account of how a little girl born blind went through a terrifying series of operations to regain her sight. The main fashion features told readers how best to spend £50 on clothes and 'how to wear the new see throughs without blushing'. Mary Grant's problem page had queries about masturbation, infidelity, and the fears of a career woman about facing a companionless middle age. There was also a 'men's postbag' revealing one male lonely heart with the isolation problem once thought to be a woman's prerogative.

Both magazines have a lively look and a positive approach. No gloom and doom, but no revolution either. Ten years, nay twenty years on, the old formula is intact even if circulation is down. It has broadened, of course, the language is less sugared, the vocabulary more sophisticated, and there is less talking down. But it is still clear that if you want circulation in seven figures, friendly persuasion and promises still works better than warnings or a call to the barricades.

Part Two

Problems and Prognostications

Money for Jam?

> We must admit that capital has been very successful in hiding our work. It has created a true masterpiece at the expense of women. By denying housework a wage, and transforming it into an act of love, capital has got a hell of a lot of work almost for free, and it has made sure that women would seek that work as the best thing in life.
>
> Silvia Frederici *Wages Against Housework*
> (Pamphlet 1974)

> The other day I was at the hospital and I went to pay my bill. This nurse came and gave me the green card. Green card is for welfare. She went right in in front of me and gave it to the cashier. She said 'I wish I could just stay home and let the money fall into my lap.' I felt rotten I was just burning inside. You hear this all the way around you. The doctor doesn't even look at you. People are ashamed to show that green card. Why can't a woman just get a check in the mail : Here this check is for you. Forget welfare. You're a mother who works.
>
> American Housewife quoted by Studs
> Terkel in *Working* (Wildwood House 1979)

There is at least one woman in Britain who is sure that she has come up with the correct formula to relieve the housewife's bondage. Selma James believes simply that women should be *paid*, by the state, in recognition of their servicing role to the whole of the nation. Most feminists are against the notion of such a payment (which has never yet come near to being a reality) because, they believe, it would merely tie women, even more than the supplementary benefits (welfare) system does at the moment, to their own apron strings.

The establishment isn't for it either. Katharine Whitehorn,

joking, made a serious point when she wrote that in her view the main argument against being paid for housework, was that she would actually have to do it and perhaps be subject to inspection. Most house-working women have that obligation already without being paid, so let us consider the arguments of Selma James.

She is a fifty-six year old black (or rather pale brown) woman from Brooklyn, very thin, speaking with high pitched drawling emphasis: she knows the answers. She was married first to a factory worker and second to C. L. R. James, the distinguished West Indian historian. She has lived in Britain now for about twenty-five years. Apart from the Wages For Housework Campaign, which she founded eight years ago, she is involved also with the Women Against Rape (WAR) campaign, one of the few really strident groups in Britain, with Prostitution Laws Are Nonsense (PLAN), the prostitutes campaign for reform, and assorted other cells, some concerned with the position of black women in Britain.

Selma James lives in a paper-strewn flat in Willesden, North West London, so packed with her own and her former husband's books that very little housework would be possible without causing an avalanche. Crouched cross-legged by her gas fire, the phone at her feet, she had her say.

Wages For Housework was founded in 1972, the year of the great Miner's Strike and also the year of one of the first big women's liberation conferences in Britain. The latter was held in Manchester and, says Selma James, it was the most exciting conference she has ever attended. Out of it, as she recalls, came two ideas – that women must join unions and that they should get Wages For Housework.

'In the early seventies, I saw the women's liberation movement as a tremendous social force which was not geared to the great social events that were taking place. And I thought we had to do that, we had to be part of those things, that we had something to say in the world which was being transformed. I never felt that our autonomy, that is our meeting without men, was only because men were intimidated women or vice versa. It was because women had to get power together and fundamentally,

66

it was going to be the organization of that women's power which was going to change the relationship between the sexes.

'I didn't have to choose between whether capitalism was the enemy, or men were the enemy. I saw the ways capitalism used men against us; and I didn't have to choose between the two extreme factions of feminism. That is, the Maoists on the extreme left and the separatists on the other hand, who were saying that men were the enemy and that if you had a male child you were selling out. I have a son (he's thirty years old now) and I definitely don't feel I had to sell out to raise him. I had another alternative, shared by very few women, which involved that vital linking of women's liberation into the great social changes we felt were taking place.

'I had gone back to the United States in 1969 and had been drawn into a picket line for welfare mothers who were saying that they wanted money from the government; that left a great impression on me. I had gone through nine weeks in the US looking for the sixties and I found the sixties there on the welfare line, in Detroit.

'I was also in contact with single mothers here in Britain, who were fighting the cohabitation rule, and I knew that those women were right. I also saw that women's liberation somehow saw the single mother and her fight as being outside the liberation struggle and I couldn't put the pieces together.

'I said I would write a paper for the 1972 conference, about our autonomy and unions and all that. We were being told that in order to fight the class struggle we had to join the unions. I knew what the unions were, and I knew that a lot of people knew fuck all about them. They had never experienced the unions as I had, both as an assembly worker and as a wife.

'The day drew nearer and I still had not written the paper. Then one week before the conference I sat down at my typewriter and wrote, "Women the Unions and Work" in three hours. A woman who was working in a factory and living in my house came home from work and read it and said, "It's not bad but it needs some demands." It was very clear to me that what women needed was money. I actually wrote the phrase "Wages For Housework" in that pamphlet.

'The conference itself was wonderful; there was just an explosion of ideas. Like talking about our mothers. I mean, I hadn't heard a lot about that except cussing mothers out, right? I was not the only mother in the movement; I was an older mother, but there were younger mothers who started to speak about that experience then.

'When I walked out of the conference I was convinced that the other five demands on my pamphlet were *all* for wages for housework; it was all the same thing. I came home exhausted, but by Tuesday I was calling people and saying, "something magnificent has happened;" and they were saying, "yes wasn't it just fantastic." And I said "listen, all of our demands are one" and I began to understand what wages for housework was. We say it's a demand and it is there, in the pamphlet, but by the time that conference was over it was becoming a political perspective. That is what it has been for us. It is a way of viewing world, of seeing how to change it. We went from a demand to a per-spective, to a strategy which is some thing different again. After you decide what you want, you have to decide how to get it.'

At this point Selma James got together, by accident she says, with three other women, all from different countries. They formed themselves into what was called The International Feminist Collective, with aim of propagating the idea of wages for housework in their own countries. That is still going on, especially in America.

'There was a period of about two years during which groups began to form. A debate went on in the women's movement, and between the left and ourselves because we were *not* the left and they hated our guts. I could show you the document that the Maoists wrote – sixty pages of it – called the Plight Of The Reactionary Selma James.

'You see, fundamentally, what the whole of left had been say-ing was what a good part of the right had been saying too: if you want to be liberated, leave home and get another job. They did not, however, say that when we got back home in the even-ing, all the housework would be waiting for us. Speaking for myself I had always wanted to get away from this second job, whether it was being my husband's secretary or working in an assembly line or in a typing pool. I knew what those women on

68

the assembly line felt like. We were all different but we all had the same aspiration – to get out of this hell-hole.

'Some would have been delighted to be on a board of directors on which they were obviously *never* going to be. Some wanted to be at home with their children because they were worried to death about what was happening when they weren't there. You are constantly thinking about the housework and the children. You worry about who the children are with, did they get the key to the front door, did they lose it and are standing out in cold? Me, I worried about the toilet training. I was terrified about complexes, right? I wanted to say what my little boy's toilet training would be like, but that right was taken away from me because I had to be on the assembly line. All of us wanted to fix up our homes, but we did not want to be slaves to a house. We wanted to go home with money.'

What, though, of the middle class housewife? Is it not indeed reactionary to suggest that she be *paid* to stay at home in already comfortable purdah? In spite of her assembly line memories, Selma James has not forgotten the kind of woman who may be married to a man flying high as a manager in a big corporation, which pays him well as it works him back into the ground, always with the assumption that the wife is there with the safety net at the bottom. With some such companies, it is even rather frowned upon if the wife has a job; it might undermine her role as her husband's other half. The large salary takes her into account, and she gets her share in terms of a nice house and nice clothes, and perhaps a car.

'First of all,' says Selma James, 'you have to find what all this means. Middle class women often employ someone else to do the housework, or part of it. The housewife does the things that interest her, and she has more flexibility. But I have been the wife of a distinguished historian, my dear, and you can't be more middle class than that. Making dinner and sitting politely for the publisher and his wife – you can take it and shove it – it is *very hard work*. I didn't make a very good deal when I exchanged the assembly line for an intellectual. I don't think there was too much to choose between them. I don't think that I worked less hard in the second situation. And I did not feel with the women I met, the wives of the publishers, and the writers, that there was any class line between us, whether or not *they* had come from the assembly line – and most of the time they had not. I didn't feel that there was any yawning gap, and they didn't either. That's very important, because although the nature of my housework changed, the fact that I was doing housework did not.

'The classic example of all this is Mrs Trudeau. I think she is splendid, she spilled all the beans at once. The woman said, "I don't want to be the rose on my husband's lapel." It's a lot, lot of work to be that. You have to be sure the petals don't wilt. I was the wife of the Secretary of the West Indian Federal Labour Party, the editor of the Nation newspaper, and I hated the time that I had to go to the hairdresser and dress up. I DIDN'T WANT IT. IT WAS A LOT OF WORK.'

Selma James believes that giving money to women, whose trouble in some cases almost seems to be too *much* money, would help: 'I'll tell you why. First of all there are not a lot of women who have enough money to support themselves. But let us take the women who do. There is no woman, not even the Queen of England, who can escape the identity of housewife. I don't know if the Prince rapes her, but I wouldn't be surprised. How can she be seen as other than a sex object? If all of us are like that, can she be different? Can she find a man who will look at her differently from the way he looks at the rest of us just because she puts a crown on her head? When I was a very young woman, I realized that the career women around me, who were not for the assembly line or the typing pool, were not any less immune to degradation than I was and were much more furious about it than I was.

'Money had blinded them to a very basic and obvious fact, that they were *women* and were going to be treated as such, and nobody was going to treat them any differently as long as they pushed me, the working class woman, around. At that I did not make the connection, I just thought they were foolish.'

It's not that Selma James thinks that these women could be helped by being *given* more money; they will have to fight for it, she says, and in the process of fighting they will have to join the people.

'That will be the beginning of the end of that kind of imposition on women, because if women are not isolated from each other, not ghettoized by the income of the man, then a whole set of things happen which in the Marxist jargon is called "an historical process". People don't grasp their own history; they don't grasp the leaps in their own mind and what caused them to take place. Women in favourable positions think that they've got there because of their own unaided efforts.

'You cannot see a movement for money, and the money itself, as being disconnected. Take, for example, the women who went along to the National Council for One Parent Families to ask for more money. They were discussing what a low image women have of themselves – and it's all our own fault actually – when a woman got up and said that, maybe we do have a low image of ourselves, but what kind of image does the government have of us, to give us this to live on? She brought the house down. We have developed our own image of ourselves from what we have seen in the mirror.'

Selma James knows that she is confronting a society which is very rigid: the people who step out from under the conventional umbrella (and more and more people are stepping or being pushed) can get into dire trouble. It isn't so much that the government thinks that women on their own are rubbish, or immoral; it is just that if they are suddenly single mothers or deserted wives or disabled persons they are outside the norm and therefore out in the cold.

'The rose covered cottage with 2.2 children stinks and the women inside it know it. Of all the women whose fight is muted, it is that woman's fight. The reason she stays there is because she doesn't have another social milieu to go to and the milieu in which she is trapped makes a judgement on her based on the statistical norm.'

Nevertheless, The Wages For Housework campaign is well aware that many of the women it seeks to liberate from rose covered cottages are less than enthusiastic at the prospect. 'People respond very defensively if they feel they are undermined,' responds Selma James undaunted. It is very important to make a distinction between the work and the person who does it, between housework and housewife.

'When we made the definitions in the beginning, we said every

71

woman was a housewife, and that includes you, and the Queen. And we defined housework as the reproduction of *people* rather than the reproduction of *things*. We defined it in the emotional sphere, letting someone cry on your shoulder, kissing the child who had hurt his knee and so on. We also defined it as sexual. It was very clear that sex was work – women were selling it, the oldest profession in the world. Sex was a big part of the expectation a man had when he married. That didn't mean that the woman didn't like it, or didn't like it sometimes. I know a lot from speaking to Mums' groups: after the meeting is over the discussion really begins. They know what is expected of them and they'll do it, but it is not what they want. Just like they have food on the table, they have to have sex in the bed.

'The women's movement has always talked about us having to determine our own sexuality. We want to decide what is happening in bed, whether we are in bed with men or with women. We want to know how, and whether it is going to be in two rooms or in five, and whether the baby is going to be in the same room at the same time. There are all kinds of ways in which we *do* determine our own sexuality, but we haven't a clue what our sexuality is; we don't know. The process of liberating ourselves is by refusing what has been thrown on us. If you say "no" you are being negative to be positive.'

Is not sex hard work for men? 'Yes and no. It is work for them in that increasingly things are demanded of them by women. But it is not work for them because generally men look to sex for pleasure and self-gratification and women help them along and very often fake the orgasms.'

I pointed to the women I knew, myself included, who enjoy sex and who might actively seek it. In the natural ups and downs of a relationship it would seem like work sometimes and pleasure at other times. Fair exchange is possible with someone you love, surely, at least in bed?

Selma was adamant. 'It comes down to conjugal rights. A man expects it, and can have it when he likes and how he likes and you are very lucky if you are with a man and the way he likes it is the way you like it too, otherwise you have to do a lot of work telling him what to do so that you can enjoy it.

'Then you face all kinds of resentment which creates a lot of

72

other housework. You have to make meals and smile a lot so he doesn't feel undermined and you are not a ball-breaker. You are a castrating woman if you demand something for yourself in bed. We are cast out if our sexuality is not available for men as society says it should be. I'm not saying that men enjoy it this way. I don't think that a rapist really enjoys life. I have spoken with women who have been raped in the street, and after the initial fury has died down, they say "You know, he really was in a terrible state."

'To be a shock absorber is a very crucial part of housework. Not only are we shock absorbers in the family, but we are shock absorbers for the crisis. With the financial situation as it flared up in the early seventies, the government launched a massive attack upon women, the biggest since the Second World War. It has really meant that our work at home has doubled. The men bring home less "real" money, we do a lot more emotional housework, we sometimes do more sexual housework. We do more child care, we are thrown out of wage earning jobs and do the same jobs at home for free. We do it silently because that is what we are trained to do and the neighbours help us a little bit. Jill Tweedie once wrote about just how much work that network produces. She pointed out that with the financial crisis, this has doubled. We have paid for the crisis on our backs, as women.

'When we were talking a lot about this in '74 and '75, other organizations were sending out pamphlets about how the working class was suffering and sometimes they talked about how babies were suffering. But how women were suffering did not come into it. The fact that housework has doubled has just not been noticed because it is not waged. Because it is not counted as work, people could not see that it was an integral part of the State's plan. We were absorbing the financial crisis. Wages for Housework really began to make a fight about that; women realized they had to fight against paying for the crisis.'

Of course housework is like that: people do not notice when you wash the dishes and dust the room and hold up the economy. They notice when you are not doing it. What then of those objectors to wages for housework who say that payment would mean obligation?

73

That, says Selma James, presumes that women clean the house and have sex with their husbands because and when they want to and don't when they don't. 'I believe that a slave often apologizes for slavery by saying "I love it". The slaves in the South used to have fights about who had the better master. *I* presume that we have to do housework because we don't have the money to say no. You can't ask me if £10 or £11 a week will make any difference. There is also a power relation between men and women which determines our behaviour, and the standards that are imposed on us. That is why the money has to come from the State, not from the husbands. The husband is going to have to go and shout at the boss instead of me. That would be a distinct improvement in relations between men and women.'

Many women surely, even if their housework was given job status and the State became the employer, would still hate the isolation of living in a house all day, cleaning it and guarding the children until the man came home? Selma James says, yes it still would be slavery, but the women would have the money to choose, to walk out. She envisages a flat rate stipend paid to all women so that there would be no question of the wages being stopped if she decided to go and do her housework elsewhere.

So, what wages for housework will buy, in effect, is the freedom to walk off the job, to withdraw labour. Selma James recalled the 1978 Ford strike in Britain, when the main point at issue was a penalty clause which said that if a man did not come in on time every day, he wouldn't get his increment. 'So you mean to say,' asked Selma, ironic, 'that as men get more money they take more time off work, they come in late more often and they do less? Very interesting. Women too. I think that as soon as we get money in our hands we buy a washing machine. I think when we get more money we buy a dishwasher. And I think when we get a lot of money in our hands we get another woman in to do it for us. It is clear that the money we have got until now has been used to cut down our housework. So the more money we get the more we'll cut it down. And I don't think that the government will be taking the children away in custody cases because we have less money than men to provide what they need. That's all bullshit because the person who is going to look after the child for the man is his mother or his sister or his new wife. Well he won't be able to do that any more, because they will have money too. No woman will be alone.'

It is still a tradition in many working class households for the man to hand his entire wage packet to his wife on a Friday. Does doling it out again not represent formidable economic power?

'That woman never takes money for spending herself. She serves herself last. As far as I am concerned there are pros and cons in that system. I was married to a factory worker. He handed me the cheque every Friday night. But that didn't mean there weren't any financial battles. He wanted a better car, and he wanted me to give him the money for the better car. A car to me didn't matter as long as it got him to work every day . . . it was an enormous amount of work to me to take his pay and make it work. My second husband wasn't like that at all. He paid all the bills and sometimes he didn't until they almost cut us off and I realized what was going on.

'All I know is that if there is not enough money, there is a lot of unhappiness. My mother always used to say "when bills come in the door, love flies out the window." I didn't know what she meant until I was married. It became a question of what were the necessities and what were the luxuries. What *he* wanted were the necessities and what *I* wanted were the luxuries. I have noticed ever since that men and women within the same relationship have two standards of living. That is a universal law. I would like it broken, OK? If *she* wants a pair of shoes, she worries about it; if *he* wants a pair of shoes, he buys them. There are women who are very extravagant but in general it is the man's will that determines how the money will be spent. Whether or not they hand us the paycheck is not really decisive.'

The Wages for Housework campaign does not deny that women live in varying positions socially and economically. 'For one woman,' says Selma, '£10 a week is a great deal and for another it is nothing. But if you get £10 a week, then presumably I would. If I don't ask for it for you, who already have good salary, then I'm much less likely to get it. It is all about women getting together and fighting. And the question of bringing women together is also the question of bringing men together.

There is a network of organizations called Payday, which fights against all unpaid work. They see Wages For Housework as the only salvation for themselves. They are not going to cease being batterers and rapists and foremen in the home until we, the women, have money of our own.

'If the State were to give us all, say £10 a week, society would not be transformed but there would be some major transformations. I know that there are women who stay with men because they have absolutely nothing; if they had their own £10 they wouldn't stay. That in itself would be a big social movement.

'And those women who have depression – the solution is not tranquillizers, it is money. The assumption that these women are depressed by staying at home. Then again you see advertisements in the medical journals depicting the over-burdened working woman carrying a shopping bag. Women like that are depressed because they have two jobs. They are being slaughtered. They are simply overworked. So, if you say women are depressed by the second job, and they are also depressed by staying home, then you have revolution. You have wages for housework.

'Eventually the government will say something like "Selma James, you were wrong starting this campaign, but I suppose there is something in what you say." So we'll get an allowance that has a fairly patronizing name. First we'll get it, then we'll change the name.'

Selma James and her followers are optimistic in the face of little apparent progress. They work hard at propaganda, and, particularly with the Women Against Rape campaign, have used the media quite successfully. How far they have reached the hearts and minds of women is questionable. 'I know there are millions of women who don't know about us, but there are millions who do. I know because I hear them on the radio. I heard one recently in a phone-in discussion about the financial battering and having a wage and getting out and escaping from it.'

Selma James herself is optimistic because, she says, you have to be. 'You can't build an international network of organizations by being a wild-eyed prophet. It has to work because other women are feeding you with their own perceptions and their own needs. And unless your power within your own life (which we call a wage too by the way) is going up all the time, you can't say "I got my wages today". A wage is not just money; it is all the things you don't have to give unless you want to and all the things you get that they don't want you to have.

'We said, how do we develop ourselves? We didn't have much time or money, which is what political development is dependent on. You cannot organize without money which is why women are in such a mess. We're the ones who have jumble sales and cake sales. Men don't have jumble sales and cake sales. They have a wallet and they pull it out.

'We never intended to be a shaking-up shocking campaign. But obviously we have had that effect. I shout and stamp occasionally because that is the way I was brought up. I'm from Brooklyn and my father was a lorry driver and my mother was a factory worker. I'm not a soft spoken middle class woman; but there are all kinds of women within the campaign. What we have never said is that the housewife is a *fool* for doing housework. We refuse to divide ourselves from other women. And our major thrust is not for recruitment, it's to raise the level of women's power and the level of women's capacity to fight.'

Selma James paints a picture of revolution a million miles from the world that we have. She acknowledges daily defeat, but counts her victories like blessings and waits for her day to come. Her Utopian vision depends on all women identifying with each other, every woman admitting to the name of housewife. Her emphasis, which most feminists would endorse on the sense of identity and *self* importance, is vital. But it is hard to see how a few pounds a week would really help the most trapped women. How, I find myself wondering cynically, would the worst husbands set about knocking a hole in this new confidence?

I recall one who, when his wife received her first child benefit book with delight, sat down and worked out how much it was costing him in tax for her to have it. And made her pay back the difference. When later this same woman got herself a low paid job, he insisted that she ever after pay for half of everything they did, even refusing to go on holiday unless she paid her own expenses. This couple eventually got divorced. The woman is making her own and her children's way in the world frugally but happily; he has bought himself a new glamorous penthouse. Everyone says he looks ten years younger.

Certainly, some kind of benefit that was not locked into the man's income would be a welcome change. Supplementary benefits which help so many women to raise their children are subject to all kinds of rules and conditions the most notorious of which is the cohabitation rule. That says in effect that a single mother receiving supplementary benefits will lose benefit if she forms a sexual relationship with a man. Once she starts cohabiting, be it only with a beggar the man is assumed to be *in loco uxor* and therefore responsible for the woman's upkeep. The kind of snooping that goes on in these cases is well known; the whole system serves to keep a woman out of the mainstream of life, rather than helping to draw her back into it.

It is the crudest illustration of the crude fact that in Britain now, men are still expected to take on a woman and to maintain her. It will take very munificent wages for housework to break that tradition.

Lonely Hearths or Splendid Isolation?

Memnon, Memnon, that lady
Who used to walk about amongst us
With such gracious uncertainty,
Is now wedded
To a British householder.
Lugete, Veneres! Lugete Cupidinesque!

Ezra Pound, Ladies, from Lustra 1916

Since Betty Friedan and before, isolation has been recognized as
the central problem of the modern housewife. But until the
arrival of the consumer age and the rigidly nuclear family, both
of which were to some extent made possible by the development of efficient birth control, the average woman's difficulty
was probably the very opposite. The mothers of the nineteenth
and early twentieth centuries can scarcely ever have had a
moment alone. Quite apart from the large numbers of children,
and larger numbers of confinements, there would have been em-
ployees, neighbours, customers (a lot of work was done at home,
even after the industrial revolution which so savagely wrenched
women workers away from their homes and relations) single
sisters, and daughters, grandmothers and so on. It would have
been a female dominated society but it would have been varied.
All the same, sometimes the married woman at the centre of it
might have envied some of the 'aloneness' of her unmarried
sisters. At the same time, a spinster, even with a place in a
crowded household, starved in the sight of plenty if she had no
husband of her own.

Today it's quite the other way : the single woman of resource
has access to all manner of social life, education and entertainment, while the isolated woman is the young mother with

babies – tied to her house – whether it be a high rise horror, or a pretty suburban semi with roses round the door, for years of her young life.

The woman's movement has been, appropriately, a lot to do with the rights and wrongs, privileges and penalties of being single. The answer to women who have been made to live 'alone' on housing estates in tower blocks or the suburbs with commuting or pub-bound husbands has been: leave, join us, find yourself, raise your consciousness, be a sister. It is men who have dumped you in the moated grange of domesticity: you don't find it fulfilling, try something else. Some have. But there were others who, like the rich young ruler in the New Testament, went away sorrowful because he had great possessions. In this case it was the husbands who probably had the possessions or care of them. But the isolation of their wives was, if not splendid, at least safe or safeish. The system which asks an ambitious right-thinking man to slave away three-quarters of his waking life, cut off from home and children, whose existence is supposed to be the mainspring of his endeavours, also asks a woman to wait and not to weep, to content herself with the care of children who need her care full time for a short period of their lives, and the care of a house, which needs her care full time not at all.

The traditional role of 'housewife' until comparatively recently amply filled a day and a lifetime. Now what remains is largely invented. I know many women who fill their days with scouring and Hoovering will be angry with me for saying so, but housewifery is no longer a calling. The more it is mechanized and technologically revolutionized and consumerized the more a thought that a robot could do it, *should* do it, gathers weight. And the more Betty Friedan's statement, that a housewife is there simply to buy more things for the house, seems true.

There have always been leisured married women, but they in other times had other roles or 'duties' to perform. After seeing to the menus and sorting out disputes between the nursery maid and the cook, they went out to live a demanding social life which included, if the lady was respectable, good charity work. But even being a flower on her husband's lapel was hard work . . . Lillie Langtry-like poise and elegance was bought at the cost of long sessions at the dressmaker and the milliner. Wandering round Oxford Street and impulse buying once or twice a year is not the same thing at all.

The charity work was and is very important. It is fashionable to sneer at the ideas of ladies bountiful setting out to distribute largesse (nowadays they tend to stop short at collecting it) among the poor and deserving. But without that kind of voluntary activity, however unevenly it was given, the annals of Victorian England would have been even blacker than they are. The soft, if not the acceptable, face of capitalism has been a woman's; the mill owner's wife who mopped the brow from which her husband exacted sweat.

The Suffragette movement was fraught by notions of public service and duty for women; it also fostered the notion that a woman had to choose between marriage and family and a career. The fact that the First World War killed off so many men of marriageable age contrived to reinforce this view and a generation of spinsters and widowed teachers raised a second generation of girls to feel something the same.

Long after, however, in the sixties, the captive wife, so well portrayed by Hannah Gavron, was caught between her education and her housework and her new dream of personal fulfilment. Good works were not enough to answer this. 'What about *me*?' asked the middle class young woman who had been told she could do anything and be anything. Until she was twenty-one, that is, at which age she married and was told she could be a mother and a house cleaner for the duration. She was too well brought up (usually) and too intelligent not to realize that there were thousands worse off than herself; but she was too much part of the system, subconsciously sold on the stream of a providing husband, lovely children and a nice house, to break free. All the same she wanted something else to do besides watch TV beside a semi-comotose man every evening. (Erma Bombeck, the American housewife-comedienne wrote that she was going to have her husband declared legally dead, he watched TV so much.)

The only day-time company to which a young mother-house-wife usually has access, is other women in the same boat. And that does not always appeal – in fact it tends to increase a feeling of detachment from the real world. A teacher who was expecting her first baby recalled walking home from school in the afternoon and suddenly noticing that all the prams were parked outside one house. It was a different house each afternoon but otherwise there was no variety. 'I suddenly had a vision of myself, sitting round with them every afternoon, talking about nappies and complaining about my husband. And I began to really *fear* motherhood.'

It needn't be, and isn't always like that of course, but the vacuum (sic) created in the suburban woman's life by the historical developments I have mentioned, is a yawning abyss for too many. It was one from which the women's liberation movement in part arose and answered with consciousness raising which has, like bra burning, some strange myths attached to it. The image is of groups of grim faced, men-hating women sitting round talking about orgasms and plotting to picket the Reform Club. In fact women's groups in Britain have tended to help members in various areas to create a sense of community in the 'vacuum' and to get away from inward looking chat merely to pass the time. But women's liberation *is* revolutionary and seeks to redistribute both emotional and financial wealth to change the male dominated culture we live in.

There are a number of other attempts to answer the isolation problem *within* that system. Most notable of these has been the National Housewives Register. It started after Betty Jerman wrote an article about the sense of isolation women felt on housing estates. A reader replied and suggested that a register of housewives right across the country would help to solve this. When a woman moved following her husband, she would immediately have access to friends and neighbours. From that started a snowball that now is a roster of more than 20,000 names from Aberdeen to Devon. I met four of them, from different groups, over coffee and biscuits in the rather formal dining room of Lisa Jones, a member of a group in Victoria, London.

Mrs Jones, who has her own business and is married to an actuary, started with the NHR out of a babysitting group: 'We had some women in the group who wanted to do more than just look after the children. Quite a lot of the people already had some sort of outside interest. A lot were beginning to feel rather trapped after having had good jobs before the children. We joined so that we had some sort of link with people in other parts of the country, instead of being just a small local discussion group. We started from scratch here five years ago; there wasn't a group before. It's very much a transient area, and our members change very frequently. A lot of people have moved away and then got in touch with their local NHR group. We have a meeting once a month but that's only in fact ten times a year. We skip the middle of the summer because too many people are away and we have a Christmas party where we allow the men.'

Lisa explained that the meetings vary quite a lot. 'We sometimes have an outside speaker come in, and then it's a case of them talking on their subject and us asking questions, rather than discussion. When we're on our own we know the topics in advance and it may be something that people want to do some research about – reading a book for instance – or it may be a subject which most people have views on and a lot of homework isn't necessary. We had a woman come to speak to us from the Marriage Guidance Council about their work, how they train people and so on. We had a recent discussion without an outside speaker about the influence of television on children. That was one where I think most people have a view. Our subjects vary. They're not all home-orientated subjects. We had a discussion on Amnesty International, because the husband of one of the members is the secretary of the local branch. We also have discussions on different areas of work and employment where we rope in friends or brothers or whatever. We had an evening, for instance, talking about what a patent agent does – how the whole system of registering a patent works. Personally, I think I've learnt about a number of different areas I wouldn't have looked at left to myself. I've made friends that I wouldn't otherwise have made.'

Gill Vine is the National Organizer of NHR. She first joined nine and a half years ago. 'My second child was a couple of months old and I went to the second meeting of a fairly new group. I heard of this meeting quite by chance – I live in Chalfont St Peter – and it sounded quite different from the usual run of coffee mornings when people say, "come along and bring the baby and we won't talk about anything serious." So I thought, I'd go along and see what it was like. I went to this house, and I went in, and there were about twelve women just sitting around. The girl who was going to set up the group, had come from a group elsewhere and was a long standing NHR member, so we were very lucky because she knew what it was all about. I thought, Yes, this is what I'm looking for. It was very different from any other women's organization I had ever come across. I had found others very disappointing because they were either very formal, or just not wide ranging enough.

'After I'd been to a few meetings, I was asked, would I do something? I vividly remember this because it was on Mexico and the girl who was organizing said, "Would you do something on the politics of Mexico?" And I thought, my God, the politics of Mexico! So I went and got some books out of the library and did all my homework and wrote it all out and went along to the meeting and sat there, not hearing a word anybody said, dreading the moment when I would have to get up and do my thing on the platform. I did it and afterwards I thought, How stupid. I am a graduate, I've had a good job, I've been a pro and I've just forgotten how to do something like this. I felt incapable.'

Gill Vine's degree is in Sociology; she did personnel work for several years and public relations after that. She said she didn't miss work to begin with because 'children keep you busy and involved, and there's plenty going on.' But after a while she missed the social contact with people: 'At home you're terribly limited in the range of people you meet. I just never talked about anything serious. Your husband comes home from work – he doesn't want to be bombarded with things; he's a bit shattered, so you can't suddenly lam into him with something you've heard on the radio. My group meets once a fortnight. The average group consists of twenty-two people. It varies tremendously. Some groups consist of ninety people, with sub groups for specialist subjects and perhaps only twenty will regularly turn up for meetings. Normally we meet in people's homes although there are one or two groups which hire a hall. The essence of it is that it is informal – you are just in somebody's home.

'The NHR has provided me with something I needed. It has provided me with conversation which was very much lacking at

84

home. Most of my friends are NHR people because I found people with whom I could get on. We don't always agree on things – which is alright because it's good to have an argument – and yet we're always friends. The group really takes the place of the extended family – it's a sort of support system. Members don't generally have family nearby. If there is a crisis in your family, it will be members of the group who will help. If a child is rushed into hospital, for instance, someone will take the other children to school, do the washing, bring food in for the husband – they really take over.'

Jean Sterk was living in Cheshire when she joined the Register. She had two children within a year (they're eight and nine now) so she was 'submerged for a couple of years in nappies and bottles and so on. I didn't mind initially because I kept up sport and I kept up one or two interests that I could do by correspondence. After two years I met a friend. I was beginning to feel fidgety mentally. This friend said she was going to a meeting and, rather like Gill, I didn't quite understand what it was about – it wasn't very clear. I went with her and the discussion was so interesting (I can't remember what it was now) and I came home so frustrated because there wasn't another meeting for five weeks.

'I got very involved because after going to a few meetings, the group wanted to have a summer outing and ideas were asked for – what we might do. I thought of the idea of having a trip on the canal with a pub supper or something – that's with husbands. I went along to the next meeting with notes on how much it would cost thinking everyone else would have done something similar. Well, no one else had done a thing, you see, so that's how I got into organizing. I organized that outing, then I found I was organizing the group and that led on from one thing to another. In due course we moved South (I live in Kent now) but before that, I got involved on the national side. I started organizing group get-togethers, day conferences and that sort of thing. I felt the register filled an enormous gap. I was in personnel management, and I did some lecturing before I had the children; stopping didn't worry me for a while because I was so elated with having children that I managed to cope with everything. But after a couple of years I needed to meet other people and have adult conversation. I felt as if my mind was like a machine badly in need of oiling. It always took half a meeting to get into gear – I still feel like that sometimes. I look after new groups specifically so I get a lot out of being involved nationally. A lot of my friends are NHR members and I've made a lot of friends through it. I've gained a lot of confidence with doing so much organizing.

'What I do involves a certain amount of travelling. We have to travel to meet each other. The groups are all so different. Some are small, some large, some intellectual, some very mundane – some are very stodgy and some are very lively. They change too, if the organizer changes or one or two people move away. You can go back and the whole atmosphere and approach will be completely different.'

Jean Sterk said there were two things people say when they've been in the Register for a while. 'One is that there doesn't seem to be any bitchiness and the other is that it is so wide ranging because you can talk about anything. The WI aren't allowed to talk about religion and politics, but with us there's scope for everything. You can take part and be involved or you can sit back and let it feed you. A lot of new members with very young children come to meetings exhausted but after a while, they find they can give something back. The aim of the national work is to keep the organization alive and to help some groups because a lot of the women need to be given confidence. They often need a few tips and hints about how to organize things.'

Margaret Beston joined the Register when she was living in Maidenhead. 'This was five years ago; we had moved from London, I had just had a baby and didn't take to motherhood at all. I was twenty-nine, and very depressed and very lonely. I was living in a very isolated way in one of a group of new houses surrounded by older houses with no young people round me. Then I heard about the NHR on *Woman's Hour*. So I phoned up the Citizens Advice Bureau and got the number of the local organizer, and I've just never looked back. She came round the same evening and collected me and took me to a book evening. I was totally amazed at what I found. I walked into a room to find eight girls discussing a book. I thought I would never ever meet anyone who read books again. I was so cooped up with the baby and had no kind of intelligent contact at all. I used to meet some girls who lived nearby, but it didn't help at all because I was tired of discussing whether the babies were on solids or not. I had all that under control and I didn't want to talk about it.

'I have two children now and I'm perfectly happy with them, now that I've made this contact that I needed. You see, before I married I did languages at a Lycee and travelled and worked abroad. When I joined the Register I found that there were lots of people like me in Maidenhead. It was a very big group that had already subdivided into special interest groups. There was a book club, for instance.

'My husband wishes there was a National House Husbands Register. He thinks the idea of going out in the evening and discussing books is wonderful. The first thing he said to me when we were moving from Maidenhead to Tonbridge was, Now, have you checked that there is a group in Tonbridge? He realizes how difficult it is to make friends in a completely new area.'

The husbands of the women I met were all professional men – an actuary, a surveyor, a civil servant and a personnel manager. But the wives assured me that the membership of the Register is far from being totally middle class; it varies from group to group, and area to area.

In Victoria, Lisa Jones said, they have a very good cross section : 'people who are living in Peabody Buildings who, not being rude to them, it's not their fault, but they don't have a very good education. As a result they benefit by coming over a topic that they otherwise wouldn't. They are harder to contact and very shy to come. When they do come they need more encouragement to come the next time. But once they've got involved, they are very good at participating.'

The other three women came from semi-rural patches of the south east, but they reported that in other areas you can find 'a very working class membership'. There are other places where every house is very isolated. Those two are the extremes. The age range now, they say with satisfaction is very wide – from early twenties to sixties. 'There are spinsters too; there are some dear old spinsters in one group I know. They love it.'

A housewife, in their eyes, is any woman who wants to join. 'We've got single parents, widows, divorcees. In fact we've got

D

the odd man who comes in to groups. I don't think that's to be encouraged really,' said Gill Vine. 'It can work to the detriment of the group because it can be offputting to have a man present, unless he happens to be the speaker. But I think there are some subjects that women are happier being on their own to discuss.' One of the four did remember a group where they had a man regularly but in exceptional circumstances. He had to stay at home because of ill-health and his wife went out to work. So he comes and 'loves it'. Most groups have social evenings and this they say is where the men benefit because it is a chance for them to meet other men. 'Commuters get so little chance to meet. Men meet very superficially – hello how are you and that's that.'

The groups are free to hold discussion evenings on anything they choose. Jean Sterk reported the forthcoming list for the Sevenoaks B group: *The Good Life* – can self sufficiency and energy conservation help us to achieve this?; *Henry VIII and his wives* – an insight into their characters; *Should libraries pay authors for the use of their books*; '*Slow down, you're going too fast*' – a discussion on the pace of life today; *Debate* (an occasional thing) – 'This house believes that Britain should leave the EEC.' (Not for nothing does the NHR rent out tee-shirts to the children of members emblazoned with the legend 'My mummy has a lively mind'.)

Other topics can be more controversial; one group even had a speaker from the National Front. 'We know in advance about the subjects of the meetings and someone always does some research so we're prepared for a discussion.' But the most provoking subjects are political issues, education and perhaps abortion, although sometimes a group would decide not to tackle a subject like that because it would be too upsetting to some members. Women's Liberation isn't in itself a hot subject. A speaker from *Spare Rib* had rather 'gone over the top,' they thought.

NHR does not run encounter groups, and members are not into consciousness raising, but they do discuss sex, at least in some parts of the country. 'The further north you go it seems the more withdrawn people are about talking about sex; the Scots are very Victorian. Sometimes we have had hilarious evenings on sex and marriage – the things people talked about I am sure they would never have dreamed of sitting down and talking about anywhere else. But because they were relaxed and with people they knew, they felt they could bring out the problems and talk about them.' Death, it seems, has become popular as a topic – 'probably because it has been pushed around a bit on *Woman's Hour* and so on; the feeling grows that people should talk about it.' Gill Vine knew of one group – and it was a rotten way to be helped – but a member had died. 'She had been so relaxed, and came to meetings and she helped the group terrifically. They all benefited from being able to share this girl's illness.'

Gill Vine couldn't think of anything groups would not discuss – but they do try to keep the range wide and to keep off domestic subjects. 'We have an annual conference and lots of day conferences,' she explained. 'Any one group can decide to have a conference or a meeting. We don't have a definite hierarchy – just the national group and all the other groups scattered about. There are twelve people in the national group, although we can have up to fifteen at once. Even the national conference is organized by a group and goes from area to area. We've got a group in Abu Dhabi and we've got such a good relationship with *Woman's Hour* that they're going to visit all our eastern groups soon. We have sprung up in the most unlikely places in the last year or so. We've got a very useful girl who does overseas for us – she's travelled a lot herself. She's been to South Africa and Rhodesia and we learnt so much about the African situation from her. We heard all sorts of stories we could never have heard otherwise. She's going round groups here talking about it now which is marvellous because she's describing a personal experience. We have active groups in Ireland. America is rather difficult. People have tried but nothing much has come of it. We're going to have an international conference in 1980.'

An important part of the Register's work then is to give confidence back to women who have been at home with children for a long time. Reaching them is the first problem. Libraries have the information, but as Gill Vine pointed out, you have to know NHR exists first, to go and ask. They would all like to see clinics and doctor's surgeries having leaflets and posters about NHR in their waiting rooms. Lisa Jones says that this has happened in the Victoria area and they have got a lot of new members that way.

But, in true British spirit, the Register encourages an attitude of self sufficiency. If a woman is unhappy it is not her hard-working husband's fault; it is up to herself to keep 'busy and happy'.

'It's up to thinking women to do something with their lives. But it depends so much on one's personality and one's husband and his attitudes. The opportunities are there providing you can make arrangements, if you don't mind spending the money you earn on nannies and so on. We wouldn't say we were perfectly happy with the system, but we have accommodated to it, learned to live with it. You could say the Register creates problems sometimes because you gain confidence and then you start looking round for ways to use it. We have had incidences of women becoming better educated than their husbands and they feel threatened. One woman went home from a meeting and told her husband that being given housekeeping money was out now, and that everyone had their own accounts. He said you'd better not go to any more meetings, then, had you? A lot depends on the set up within the marriage. If the partners take equal shares in the running of the home, then the woman has free time, but if he is the kind of man who expects everything done for him, then she won't have much time on her hands. That's partly historical accident, and partly just women accepting what men demand. Some accept, and some don't, whereas in the past, more accepted.'

At the Charity Commissioner's Gill Vine arguing that the Register should have charitable status said she had had the most gruelling couple of hours of her life. 'He was trying to convince me how inward-looking we are, and I was trying to convince him that we are outward looking. For instance an awful lot of members go on to do Open University degrees after they've been involved with a group for a while. You find that most of these further education courses are full of NHR members and they've only gone back into it because of what they've been involved in in the groups. It's a stimulus and makes you feel that you can go back and do something. We push the members outwards, and help them make the best of their abilities. Once you're involved, you either forget about the things that have got you down or you learn how to cope with them.

'We do have a few vociferous members who are forever telling everyone they ought to be getting back to work and then again, there is a strong nucleus of women who are quite happy with their position. We don't aim to be a therapy group but a lot of women will say that they were depressed before they joined or would have become depressed if they hadn't joined.'

The Register provides information about a lot of possible outlets for women once they have regained their confidence. 'The newsletter contains so much information. There is a review on that book, *Going Back To Work* which is a terrifically useful little book.'

NHR would stop short of starting a campaign to change a law, or some aspect of the system, said Gill Vine. 'We can't act as a pressure group. Members can join pressure groups or start their own but they mustn't mention NHR in that context. It needs to be put on some sort of firm footing for the future and being a charity would help that. I don't think it's fair for an organization the size of this one to be run from my dining room, a room in Jean's house and a room in somebody else's house. I think eventually we might well need a centre. If we have charitable status then we could get half the rent and rates and a little back room behind a shop – perhaps near where the national organizer lives. We're waiting to hear about that. It would give us a chance to explain what we're about. Other organizations can say they provide blankets for refugees or whatever but our aims are nebulous. My son says to me, "What do you actually *do* at your meetings? Do you just sit and talk?" But my daughter has been helping me collate the circular for the last few days and she said, "I think I'll do this when I'm a mummy." So I can see her being National Organizer when she's got her own family and wants something to do.'

Nuclear Disaster, or is Matriarchy Inevitable?

If your wife is of a servile disposition and has a crude and shifty spirit, so that pleasant words have no effect, scold her sharply, bully and terrify her. And if this still doesn't work . . . take up a stick and beat her soundly . . . but notice I say that you shouldn't beat her just because she doesn't get things ready exactly as you like them. You should beat her only for a serious wrong . . .

> *Rules of Marriage* compiled by Friar Cherubino of Siena
>
> between 1450–1481

I have only half lived
I found a master
When I needed
a friend

> Karolina Pavlova (1807–1893)

There is a darker side to home life than anything admitted by the 'busy and happy' members of the National Housewives Register. Domestic violence has always existed alongside domestic bliss. A man's right to beat his wife as if she were his carpet has origins lost in the primeval mists. It had the blessing of law in England until the eighteenth century, and the blessing of popular morality until the present day. It was only in the mid nineteenth century that it became legally possible for the wife to flee the matrimonial home, and it was only two years ago (1978) that the law declared that a violent husband could be ordered out of his own house.

We have known ever since records were kept that, if you discount war, the majority of murders are domestic. In other words, committed by one member of a family upon another – 'private' crimes. Furthermore most murderers are men. Thus, if a man is not off killing the enemy he may well be killing, or half-killing, his wife, or his child or his step-child, or anyone that is his.

The modern women's liberation movement did not discover this kind of violence, which is by its very home-bound nature, often hidden and denied by both victim and practitioner. But it has, in the last decade been given a new name. Battering. As in assault and battery. As in pancakes. We have read, during the past ten years, horrifying annals of baby and child battering, wife battering, granny battering and even husband battering. The word has been somewhat displaced lately by the American term 'abuse', but battering seems to me still the better word because it is both physical and psychological in meaning, and because it implies unrelenting attack, a long state of siege. Abuse is vaguer, weedier; you abuse a privilege it is true, but you batter a door down.

There was every incentive, in the back-to-the-hearth-and-home fifties for all family horrors, including beatings, to be kept dark. But one of the first things that happened with the advent of the women's movement was that the secret was out. Where two or three were gathered together to raise consciousness, they like as not found themselves raising roof and hackles with tales of every kind of 'abuse', from burns to black eyes. Now there are around 150 refuges affiliated to the National Women's Aid Federation and a growing number of self help groups for women who have, or feel that they may, batter their children. Doctors have learned to look for and recognize the problem, and to see through the smokescreen of concealment thrown up by even the most cruelly-treated women. The battle against violent husbands and mothers and fathers is well engaged, if not by any means won.

The passionaria of this social revolution and revelation is Erin Pizzey. In 1971 she founded Chiswick Women's Aid, out of her own loneliness and feeling of being trapped as a housewife, and out of a desire to contribute something at an immediate and basic level to the women's revolution that she saw starting up around her. Erin is a blowsy mother earth; she weighs sixteen stone, and looks like a cross between the butter mountain and Boudicca. She is undoubtedly one of the most famous women in

Britain, and certainly one of the most charismatic. Her open door policy for battered women and her running battles with Hounslow Council, plus her personal eloquence, have won her the ear and the backing of rich men and poor women alike. She is branded reactionary and regressive by some feminists and resented by the Federation because, they feel, she gets too much media attention for what she does while they are ignored. But without her embarrassing, ever-articulate presence, one of the key issues of women's liberation would have had far less of a hearing than it has.

I went to ask her about violence in the head rather than in the fists, and her answer came down to one simple central thesis. She thinks that the nuclear marriage is by definition violent, and would like to see it replaced by some new community-centred society, in which men and women could be free to relate to each other as equals. 'Any one-to-one relationship between a man and a woman is potentially violent. It is a trap, and the only way that equality can be achieved is within a community setting. That way no one person could become the repository of everything the other person needs, whether emotionally, economically or for any other reason. Nobody can do it, it's totally unrealistic – and yet that is what we ask of people.'

A yearning for a tribal system pervades her thinking: 'Essentially, human relationships are very chaotic. Tribal living has a natural chaos of its own, and the way it was replaced was with order. The order has created so much violence that people are naturally reorganizing themselves into a community kind of living. Even if you take the communion that happens between the single mothers and their children living around here (Shepherds Bush and Chiswick) there are very strong relationships between them. I think that it will find a level of its own – although our society is so technical, that when that much freedom is given to a woman, it is very quickly organized and taken away by the male dominated structure. Like whoever it was saying in the House of Lords that all our economic problems could be solved if women didn't go to work. When things get threatening, whether it is under Fidel Castro or Margaret Thatcher, it's back to the cooking pots.

'The kind of violence I deal with in the refuges is raw physical

94

violence for which there are very specific causes – battered children who have grown up to batter and so on. But relationship violence is a very unsaid violence. It is the grey faced woman who has lost her sense of humour and her youth and her sense of who she is as a person. It's the man who can't cope with what is happening at home so he's never home, for every good reason in the world. He's not even necessarily having affairs on the side, he's just hanging on somewhere. "Who conned who?" they may ask themselves.'

Chiswick Women's Aid was born out of a row Erin had with her former husband Jack. 'I said, I can't stand this any more, I'm leaving, and I walked out of the house pushing Amos, who was new-born, in the pram, with Cleo, who was about five, holding onto the side. Then I suddenly realized that I had nowhere to go. That happens to so many women. So the original Women's Aid was a little house and any woman who came with her children was entitled to a key. Nobody had any idea what a revolution that was except the women who came. Because the only key you ever have is to your father's house or your husband's house. Here they could come and go whenever they wanted, it belonged to them. If I had had a key that day, I would not have had to push it until I walked out. That little house was an incredibly thriving place, and it is what the women's movement should be about – drawing women in – not in an attempt to wreck marriages or relationships but in an attempt to educate women into educating the men they are with as well. Then different relationships would be possible – not the hidden smouldering bitterness that ends up with her with her legs crossed, and him at the other side of the bed. But *real* relationships based on equality.

'I am prepared to struggle to make it possible for there to be relationships between men and women that are equal but different. I had a conversation with a woman once and she was going on about how her fellow came home from work and got on with the washing up etc. to such an extent that I ended up saying to her, "what's it like going to bed with a dishwasher?". If the sexual tension doesn't exist between a man and a woman then there really isn't any relationship. We women demand spiritual relationships with men which they find very hard, because most of their relationships function on the end of their pricks. We

95

keep saying, it's not like that but I'm afraid it is. It doesn't mean that men don't love as passionately, they just love differently : in a much more sensual, physical animal and brutal way. Not brutal in the sense of violence, just more raw.

'Every time I meet a man who says "I'm a feminist" I think my God I don't trust you. Because they've sussed it and they are usually the most violent. I have seen women out-houseworked by their husbands and been worse off. I think that there is something very dangerous about trying to make men into women. Men are men and women are women and men very rarely want children. When you try to get the man in your life to share what is really your side of mothering what you are going to do is confuse the children as to what is male and what is female.'

The grind of caring for small children is frequently blamed for the trapped feeling experienced by many women. Erin Pizzey thinks differently : 'The burden is psychic. Caring for the children or doing a job are not the burdens. It is trying to be all things to all people that makes a woman end up with a totally splintered ego, a sense of being a failure all round. A woman who is running a house is doomed to failure. It is a seventy-eight hour week, for a start. There is no recognition for what she does, and the most important part of her, her thinking self, is ignored. So, she goes out to work to see if that will resolve the problem. And then she fails completely. She is constantly anxious. Is the child sick? Is the child about to be sick? There is a miasma of guilt over her whole life, so that she ceases to be a human being.

'Until the government and men in general, realize that children are the gold of our future, no status will be given to women staying at home to look after the children. I would do away with half the social services, and re-employ women at home with children.' And by 'work' she doesn't mean housework. 'A lot of women working at Chiswick have children and bring them to work. You've got, sitting at home, the most talented people on earth. And women with every kind of professional training. The most exciting thing for men in the work I have done is, not looking towards female ghettoes, because I have always worked with men, – but the discovery that a community setting is the ideal way for women to be able to explore all their talents, because then the work can be shared round. My Bristol house has five or six women in it and they have about fifteen kids between them. They have the most marvellous freedom. They are all on social security; they share all the bills and they have a common bank account. Those that work work and those who don't stay home and look after the children. It is a co-operative women's community.'

Erin's pet co-operative dream is to have women running transport cafes in a chain called Mothertruckers. That way, she reckons, women could make lots of money and not be forced into shoplifting and prostitution because they haven't got enough to live on. It is crucial, she believes, for women to be able to take their children to the workplace if they wish. 'Telling us that we can't take our children is just a way of getting rid of us, because the fact is you work just as well with your children round you. But society hates children. The only place open to children is the park, or the supermarket for ten minutes before your child is kicked out, or a library for another few minutes. If women are going to use themselves and their talents and their abilities, they have got to be permitted to have children and have them visible, and work in their own way. We have got to get rid of the male structures that make women invisible. They've *got* to accept us you know, we are half of the human race.

'I would like to break down the whole social services system and get back to women organizing themselves in their own community, which they previously did very successfully. The undeniable results of what I have done have been recognized internationally. I've proved that you can deal with the most difficult families, that no one else can manage, because we allow for chaos. We allow for chaos and allow it to reign. Women *can* allow a greater deal of chaos without fear because that's how family life is. A man is ordered from the beginning of his life. He has to achieve a career of some sort to be anybody, and he has to have order. Women, on the other hand, have this need for creative chaos. If Chiswick had been run by men, there would be a bank of secretaries in there or a front organization of some sort running it.'

Erin Pizzey finds the word 'housewife' a destructive, difficult word. Her own experience of the label and the role, before she

97

joined the women's movement and then started Women's Aid, was not happy: 'I got to the stage where I felt so demoralized that I was like some sort of cabbage. I remember going to the preview of a film Jack had made, and all sorts of trendy people were there. I met this other wife and we spent the whole evening talking about measles injections. We had nothing else to say and no one would talk to us anyway. They'd come up and say, who are you, and I'd say I'm married to Jack and they'd say, oh how interesting, what do you do? and I'd say I look after the children and they'd say how interesting, I must just go and get a drink. And that was it, they'd gone. I can remember, too, having an incredible hatred for any women who were working outside the home. I remember a woman producer telling us over dinner about how she'd left the children with a new au pair and one of them had fallen through the top banister and broken his jaw. And I, in my anger that I was at home all day and boring and ugly and unimportant, was very heavy with her. It was pure malice on my part; I was jealous. There she was, very glamorous with a smashing job and lovely house and everything. But in fact she was suffering just as much as I was and I soon realized that women have to give each other an awful lot of affection and support. It is not just a question of trapped and untrapped. Everybody's trapped.

'Almost all my friends, the ones we knew as couples, are separated, they are all single parent families. I can only think of two that aren't. But women of my generation, when I told them that my divorce from Jack was a healthy forward looking move, found that idea very difficult to cope with, I felt at one point that if one more of our mutual friends had rushed up to us and clutched my hand and said what a tragedy, they would discover themselves flat on their backs. I laugh about it with my daughter Cleo, and say that perhaps her children will be insisting on white weddings and spend their time discussing how to lose your virginity on honeymoon. There is always this pendulum.

'It is not that women are unhappy with their children, it's not that I actually hated being at home with my kids. What I couldn't stand was that I was totally isolated once I was at home with them. Before the industrial revolution, the women were the social workers and the midwives (who had much greater standing in the community then) and they did creative things at home. They made things. Now it is very different. Lenny Bruce put it beautifully when he said that "the trouble with women is that they keep looking for relationships, through men, with another woman." He didn't mean that in terms of being lesbian. He meant that we are asking men to do things that just aren't male. They are not going to be our best girl friends, or be there and talk to us every evening. My grandchildren's other grandmother is West Indian, and she thinks white women are potty. Her old man is off with his friends every evening and she has a great social life of her own with her friends. Something went badly wrong when we decided that what ought to happen is that one man and one woman should relate to each other behind one front door totally by themselves for the rest of their lives.

'In order for a man to achieve what the technological revolution asked of him, he had to devote himself full time to working and then to being home. I'm not sure whether you can pin-point when and where it went wrong but it has certainly been a disaster as far as I'm concerned. There is nothing more damaging to children than the lonely isolation their mother suffers being at home all day, and the absence of the father. He doesn't usually come home until the kids are in bed and only sees them at the weekends when he is really tired.'

Not that women are innocent of complicity in this scheme of things: 'I always say, scratch any woman and underneath is a three piece suite. But only until they have had their kids. Once they hit the labour table they know what life is all about. Until then it is all the ad-man's dream.'

Erin Pizzey was an early new wave feminist, right in there at the beginning, inspired by the writing of Jill Tweedie and hopes of a brave new world. But she feels now that it was doomed to partial failure from the outset because it was a movement imported from America and because it was too middle class. 'We got all the real extremists from the States, the weathermen, the bombers. They bombed a BBC van, I remember. It all began with tremendous hysteria, but it was quite useful in that they raised people's consciousness overnight. But we never had a chance, as Englishwomen, to relate to each other. What it did do was frighten off the whole broad mass of women in England who were desperate, who did need to hear the message and get involved. The women's movement never developed a politics of women; they merely adopted the politics of men. That is still true now.'

Erin was in fact quite quickly thrown out of the women's movement – banned from all the meetings. 'When I look back on it now it is incredibly funny. I think it is very hard for highly educated women to realize how politically naive most women are. I remember when they were trying to throw me out I managed to convene a meeting to ask why, if they were talking about "the working classes" so much, there were no working classes anywhere near the movement. I hadn't met one. And to ask why anyone who came near the movement had to have a dictionary in one hand – everything was polemic and dialectic and so on – and why we had agendas and minutes and all the things men have, instead of organizing things in a different way. They all came; thousands of women in black clothes all screaming at me. It was terrifying. Very, very heavy.

'I think an enormous amount has happened in ten years – without the movement I doubt if there would have ever been any refuges for a start – but I do think that feminism has been too exclusive. There was a party line that had to be toed, and it actually excluded about ninety per cent of women in the country who in fact believed in half the tenets that the women's movement was fighting for. Anyone who thinks a national organization is going to reach "ordinary women" is going to fail, because until you have been at home with young children and seen how damaging that can be to your self confidence you can't see that the only way you're going to get a woman to come with you is to take her by the hand and show her the alternative. That is why our key was so important. You need a place every three or four streets, but *not* run by the social services. When I went to that first big Women's meeting in 1971 it was the first time I had been out of the house without my husband in ten years of married life. Jack babysat. When I got back he said "I can see you must be very lonely sometimes."

'I don't think that it is our generation that the women's movement is going to affect so dramatically – though it certainly completely changed my life – it will be our daughters who really show the difference. There is a huge cross section of teenagers coming through here and I find that the girls are much less needing to be male-related than my generation. It is the economic thing that has done it. Social security, though it is bread line living, has made it possible for women to bring up children without depending on a man. Don't tell them that though, or they'll take it away. It has done more to emancipate women than any movement.'

One of the healthier effects of the movement, as Erin sees it, has been women's growing confidence and their growing refusal to tolerate the bad behaviour of men. 'The whole fabric of society is changing round; there is a whole female culture growing naturally on its own. One in three, or is it one in two, marriages now breaks down and the children stay with the mothers. If men aren't very careful matriarchy is going to sweep back in. Many of the girls I see will retain the father of their child as a friend or lover, but they keep their own space. The mother's name is on the birth certificate. The wind of change that blew right the way through has affected every single woman in this country in one way or another, even though it unsettled mothers in their beds – you know, my age group. The people who hear it are the children and it is very interesting that my daughter and all her friends – just going through all the hundreds of teenagers that I know – are feeling that economically it is no longer a question of just putting up with it. If a relationship is bad they have other alternatives.'

Erin's seventeen-year-old daughter Cleo caused her mother to turn in her bed more than once when she announced that she was pregnant at the age of fifteen. 'Everyone was hysterical, you can imagine,' recalls Erin. 'But in the end I said well, babies are babies and when they come, they come.' Cleo now has two children by the same father, who is West Indian. The couple remain close, but they do not live together. Cleo is still under her mother's ample wing, but she is a calm and self-possessed young woman. She recognizes that she has become a mother at the same time as growing up. Some of her friends have done the same but it hasn't worked so well for people totally on their own. Her friends plan ahead, she says, and don't take things for granted. She can't imagine living with just one person, and reckons that when she's thirty she'll be free to do other things and it won't be too late. 'Funnily enough,' she said thoughtfully, 'I do get branded as a housewife.'

As Cleo talked, Erin listened approvingly, rocking her tiny coffee-coloured grandchild Amber against her all engulfing bosom. Other assorted children and friends and dogs of various ages and colours wandered in and out. Peace, if not tranquillity, reigned. Is this a vision of the future that many of us could live up to?

I Want it Now; The Orgasmic Imperative

What is it men in women do require?
The lineaments of gratified desire.
What is it women do in men require?
The lineaments of gratified desire.

William Blake, *To God*

Whisky blind, staggering home at five
My only thought is how to keep alive.
What makes him tick? Each night now I tie
Ten dollars and his car key to my thigh . . .
Gored by the climateric of his want
He stalls above me like an elephant.

Robert Lowell, *To Speak of the Woe that is in Marriage*

Female sexuality has, time out of mind, been seen by men (and some of their wives and mothers) as a dangerous thing, to be neutralized as far as possible. There are of course different ways of achieving this. The most extreme, still followed in parts of Africa and the Arab world is the barbarous and cruel rite of circumcision of women. It is a dreadfully painful 'initiation rite' and leads to health problems and complications in child bearing that would make the most seasoned obstetrician weep. Without it, however, women in these communities have scant chance of finding a husband: an unmutilated woman is more likely to be unfaithful and, what's more, she carries the vestiges of masculinity (i.e. her clitoris). The 'operation' is performed without anaesthetic by older women upon pre-pubescent girls (it is euphemized as 'going to granny's' in the Southern Sudan) and, in its most radical 'Pharaonic' form, it removes large chunks of the genital area including the clitoris and banishes all chance of sexual sensation other than pain.

Western 'cultures' have used subtler, gentler methods to tame female ardour. In Britain we may have come a long way since the chastity belt, but it isn't so very long since the famous Victorian directive to a bride 'close your eyes and think of England'. In spite of the efforts of every sexologist and feminist since Marie Stopes we have not quite rid ourselves of the notion that sexual intercourse is a wife's rather distasteful duty, which every husband has the right to expect on demand. The woman's not to question why, hers but to endure and lie. Compensation for this submission was, and is, home, hearth, children and security.

Thus, husbands have not until recently expected their wives to actually *enjoy* sexual attentions; rather the contrary. Sexual abandon was something sought or bought elsewhere, or simply fantasized about.

Fear of the female has deep and mystic roots, as every psychologist since Freud has been happy to tell us. But there is a simple practical rational force which women well understand. It's about property, like everything else to do with marriage, declared a Belfast housewife: 'Medieval knights locked their wives up because they had to be very sure that their sons were really *theirs*. If women were allowed to develop their sexual appetites, who knows whose child might inherit the good man's earth.' Therefore right until the present days of female-orgasm-on-demand and wife swapping, men have felt safer with a woman who is closer to being a mother than a lover. Women have connived at their sexual disinheritance because it seems the only way to hold on to other advantages. Men (and women) who have hoped for romance and passion in marriage have sometimes found it, but as often have been bitterly disappointed.

One of the greatest achievements of the women's liberation movement has been to crack some of the main myths and labels of female sexuality – the bitch goddess, the earth mother, the tart, the tease, the ice maiden, the nymphomaniac. Freud's great dicta about penis envy and vaginal orgasm have been scotched; a new emphasis on the women's enjoyment has been the sexual angle on the growing faith in friendship and sharing generally.

It is not possible in this space for me to *precis* the sexual research that has helped this shift ... Masters and Johnson, Kinsey, et al. Suffice to say that in the fifties and sixties, the women of America were beginning to be asked and to *talk* about their feelings of unease and deprivation physically, and of the loneliness between two people who cannot find a common level for lovemaking. Betty Friedan found that when her housewives spoke of sex there was 'a false note, a strange unreal quality to their words.' She quoted the woman who was beginning to feel contemptuous of her husband in bed. 'I never really *feel* him.' Instead of fulfilling the promise of infinite orgasmic bliss 'sex in America of the feminine mystique has a strangely joyless national compulsion, if not a contemptuous mockery.' This was apparent in movies, books and sex guides alike. Kinsey, from his interviews with nearly 6,000 women, found that the majority had desires that their husbands could not satisfy.

I am not qualified to write a psycho-sexual thesis about frigidity, orgasm or any other aspect of sexuality. The women interviewed for this book were not grilled about their sex lives : some refused to talk about the subject at all, or even if willing, seemed to lack the language to express anything but the vaguest indications of happiness or dissatisfaction. They were not pressed. Some were probably as happy as they said, others may have had problems only a clinic could fish for.

I was in any case less interested to pursue problems of sexual technique and performance or explore the realms of sexual fantasy, than to hear what women who described themselves as 'happily married' had to say about the housewifely aspect of sex – whether they still saw it as a duty as well as (or rather than) a pleasure.

Comments revealed a conflict between an eagerness to please and placate husbands, and a longing to please themselves. If they failed to do the former, the man might leave to seek comfort with all the hundreds of eager, sexually available younger women the wives (not without reason) imagined to be hovering under every metaphorical lamp-post. If they failed to do the latter they might become doormats and 'lose' themselves and their husbands as well.

Many women showed genuine anxiety for their husbands'

sexual wellbeing. Seeing how closely virility was bound up with self-regard, they felt it was their duty to foster it in rather the same way as they would always be sure to have a good meal waiting in the evening. Even those whose husbands were evidently thoughtless and abusive sexually were defended by wives who seemed to subscribe to the ancient myth about the coarse animal appetites of men which must be appeased. Just as it has traditionally seemed dangerous to unleash women's sexuality, it has seemed dangerous to repress that of men.

The following short quotations from women were typical of those gleaned while researching this book. (They are not necessarily the words of the people quoted at length in Part III.)

'He always wants to make love just when I've got the baby off to sleep and have a chance to sit down for five minutes. I never turn him down because I don't want him to feel pushed aside. Saying I'm tired just sounds like rejection.' – Thirty year old mother of two young children.

'You're lying in bed, absolutely wiped out after a hard day with the kids, and this hand comes across. It's the last thing in the world you feel like doing but you've got to make the effort. It can be so damaging if they feel rejected – that's when they start looking for it elsewhere.' – Thirty-five year old mother of four.

'What I resent is that whatever happens he gets *some* pleasure out of it. I mean he *always* comes and it doesn't matter what I feel like. I sometimes think that all those jokes about women sending substitutes in the dark aren't so funny. He wouldn't notice. Sometimes, when he just rolls over again and goes to sleep, I lie awake and *fume* for ages.' – Thirty-six year old housewife.

'Having children puts your sex life into a bit of a rut. We used to do it anywhere in the house, any time we felt like it. But you can't make love on the sofa in the evening in case one of the children wakes up and wanders in. It's all so much more formal.' – Twenty-eight year old mother of two.

'We're lucky if we both manage to stagger home, have something to eat, collapse in front of the television and then fall asleep the minute we touch the sheets – never mind having a wild time between them.' – Twenty-five year old wife.

Complaints about tiredness and male insensitivity were somewhat balanced by happier statements.

'After the second child was born sex was a nightmare because they stitched me up badly. It was agony every time. Now I've had another baby and they've sorted out the problem and I've been sterilized so I feel totally relaxed. I'm able to have orgasms for the first time in three years.' – Thirty-two year old mother of three.

'My husband is a wonderful lover; he always seems to know when I don't feel like it. We have been married for a long time – twelve years – and we have found out how to communicate physically without being crude or pushing each other away. He doesn't mind if I make the approach either.' – Forty-two year old teacher and mother of two.

Most women still seem happy to leave the 'approaches' to their husbands, although some said that wasn't so when they first married. Some had fantasies about taking a lover, but these were vague and most said they would be frightened to do it in reality. Flirtation at parties was as far as most wanted to go. Nearly every woman interviewed said they would have been 'shattered' if they knew their husband was being unfaithful. 'You've got to believe he isn't, although I'm sure most men go astray sometime in their married life,' said the wife of a businessman. 'They are subject to so much temptation every single day. But if you sat at home worrying about what secretary was making eyes at him next, you'd go potty.'

Another woman felt that sex was not very important as a bond of marriage and that it was perhaps just as well if her husband occasionally sought entertainment elsewhere. 'I don't want to know the details, but I wouldn't try to stop him. I know he doesn't stay with me because of my sexual charms, however great they are. He stays because of the children and his enormous emotional and financial investment in the family and the marriage. And we do *love* each other.'

So, there seems to be, if it is at all fair to generalize from random interviews and conversations, a double pull on wives. First to please their husbands: 'I know how desperate I feel when he turns up his nose at my cooking. Turning up my nose at him sexually would be much the same and I wouldn't do that to him.' Second, they want some self-fulfilment and independence from the male seal of approval : 'I sometimes long to be just *me*, not just so-and-so's wife, a built in sex object and dishwasher.'

On the other hand, when the chips were down, some women reckoned that withholding sex was their best weapon : 'I know it's unfair but he won't listen to me when I try to talk about my feelings. It's only in bed, when he wants something from me urgently that I can get back at him.'

In the bad old days sex for a wife was inextricably bound up with fear of, or desire for, pregnancy – mostly the former. The letters with which Marie Stopes was showered when she pioneered birth control in the twenties and thirties bear poignant and tragic witness to that. Pleasure was mentioned only in passing and orgasms were talked of only by the 'upper classes'. A 'problem' such as 'frigidity' could have been seen as a means of contraception. Now that, and all other such psycho-sexual difficulties are regarded more as a failure of the relationship or of one or other partner thereto or a practical, physical problem. In magazines women's self sufficiency has reached a new level – we must, according to at least one recent article, 'take responsibility for our own orgasms.'

Sex is, of course, like clothes and houses and motor cars, tied up with status – both in the pecking order between husband and wife and their individual places in society. Sometimes the woman who is 'frigid' (a hateful expression that should be banned) or holds back from her husband, is punishing him in some way for where he has placed her, or for what he stops her from becoming. She is hanging on to the only part of herself that he can't have unless she does offer it. When he forces himself on her, or she 'submits', then it is a technical rape within marriage; some couples live in this bizarre uncomfortable state of siege for years.

The man – on whom this situation can be hard – can only blame himself. He has, albeit with her eager connivance, penned his lady within the moated grange of domestic life. Refusing his attentions is one way she has of showing what she feels about it that doesn't show in public, but can be cruelly undermining behind the scenes.

Some of these difficulties end up on the psychiatrists couch or in the sex clinic – a new development for Britain. Ten years ago there were no psycho-sexual clinics in Britain. Now there are more than 100 – run by the NHS, the FPA, various private trusts and the National Marriage Guidance Council, who were pioneers with the methods of Masters and Johnson the famous American sex therapists. To oversimplify, this treatment allows the 'patients' to work out their problems physically in the clinic with a counsellor who can play the role of a surrogate sex partner. It is no longer simply a question of talking through often unexpressible difficulties.

A woman who rejects her husband in bed while loyally cooking him steak and kidney pudding downstairs, may openly talk about her inability to come to orgasm with him. But she is not always eager to solve the problem which might lose her some power, or worse, put the whole structure of her life in jeopardy. Often such talk is (and self confessedly so in the case of some women) punitive – a reminder to a man that he can't have everything just because he has the money.

Counter to this runs the feminist concern over 'rape within marriage'. The notion that a man owns his wife physically and has conjugal rights over her is time honoured and lives still. But for every insensitive brute bludgeoning his way willy nilly into his wife's body against her will and dignity, there may be a puzzled frustrated husband longing to please his wife but finding his own potency and self regard smashed beyond repair in the attempt. It is very difficult to change a pattern of behaviour or interaction of this sort and it may only be an outsider such as a therapist or a trauma such as another affair for one of the partners that will do the trick for better or worse.

Many women are still prepared to put sexual problems aside but they do figure more and more in the reasons for divorce. This is not to suggest that people part simply because they don't indulge in sexual gymnastics each night, or because the quality of the woman's orgasm is inferior. But without a wholesome sexual communication, as one psychologist told me, it is very difficult for people within a marriage to solve other difficulties.

'Making up' after a quarrel, for instance, is very hard without physical love. Also, if one partner feels undervalued by the other, his or her self valuation tends to drop. A man can bolster his more easily – secretaries, barmaids, other women in the outside world are always available, if not for a full blown affair at least a nice chatting up.

Women do not find it so easy to seek consolation elsewhere when they are rejected at home: 'I've gone off sex, I don't know why and I don't want to discuss it,' one thirty-five year old husband announced to his thirty year old wife, as he firmly turned his back on her. He kept it turned for several years before they finally got a divorce. During that period his wife, a fully qualified nurse among other things, said she lost all belief in her own attractiveness and value in the world.

Sex in marriage has always been so bound up with the begetting and bearing of children – even wedding and honeymoon jokes are all about troubles being little ones – that the pleasure and fulfilment aspects have been regarded as secondary. If children were to be kept safe, the less sexy a wife felt, the better it would be. Thus the new admissibility of female sexuality is very threatening to the traditional power structure of marriage.

Paul Brown, a clinical psychologist who has concentrated on psycho-sexual problems, and has worked for the Marriage Guidance Council in the establishment five years ago of their sexual dysfunction programme (based on Masters and Johnson techniques) has noted some dramatic changes, especially in the last two years. For instance, people's level of information about themselves and their bodies and their sexual problems has risen. Brown takes questions on these matters on a local radio call-in show and reports a marked increase in callers' readiness to talk frankly, and ask questions in an informed and precise way. Things have got to the point, he declares, where the general public is better informed about sex than the medical profession. 'Doctors don't listen to their patients; they fob them off with tranquillizers.'

Brown can produce a hair-raising history or two to prove his point. There was a woman with a pain at the entrance to her vagina during intercourse, for instance. She went to a well known gynaecologist who could find nothing wrong. She said well, the fact is I am experiencing pain. He said well, just let's call it buttercups and daisies. When he heard, Brown was so angry he sent her to a specialist in sexual function who discovered that, in a state of sexual arousal, small vaginal warts became visible. That was where the pain was coming from.

'There are also all the women who present with back pain, or thrush or cystitis. The GP never asks – he just treats them as a straight physical problem,' said Brown. 'Sex is very threatening for doctors; they only know what they have experienced themselves. They ignore the sexual component of a patient. The law and codes of practice are all designed to defend doctors against the notion that they are interested in the patient sexually. This is strange because medics feel they have the right to stimulate any other situation: they flash lights in your eyes, they pump stuff up into your gut, they peer into your ears.'

Brown pointed to the lack of sources of information for the medical profession: 'They have really only got *Forum* magazine and the *British Journal of Sexual Medicine*. There is just beginning to be a professional literature. The popular press on the other hand talks very straight forwardly on the issues (the magazines, the *Daily Mirror*). It may be billed as love, but it's sex they're on about. So, the public are better informed, but still ascribe all kinds of mystique to doctors. All the time they themselves know more intuitively, and more in fact.'

People can, according to Brown, endure years of misery because there is nowhere they can turn for practical, informed help. Their very real difficulties may be nothing to do fundamentally with the relationship. 'We have to sophisticate GPs. The patients may not be able to properly explain themselves. But repeated presentation with the same complaint without any apparent cause may simply mean that the patient needs to be asked the right questions.'

Men too have a lot to learn. 'The standard English male thinks of a woman like an umbrella,' Brown declared. 'It opens up when he wants, accompanies him when he wishes and can be put aside when he wants. But it is always there ready for use. When the umbrella says hey, I'm a person, the "owner" feels impelled to get it under control and shut it up in some other way.

'In sex, men are supposed to know, women know that they

don't know, but can't let them know they know ... terrible double bluff goes on. I have terrible renegade views of the whole development of Freudian theory, which is really a phallic-centred theory. There is a massive unrecognized defence to that, which is that women now hardly need men: they can reproduce, feed, do everything unilaterally. Now that they can cut men out of conception process with AID, men are redundant. I think that men have cottoned on to that at a subconscious level.

'Another aspect of the process towards self-sufficiency is the development of a really reliable contraceptive. Up to the mid thirties the sexual act was almost entirely linked to procreation; any pleasure was accidental, a bonus. From the mid thirties to the fifties (which coincided with the formation of the MGC and the Catholic counselling advisory service) the popular view of sex stemmed from Hollywood. There was a relationship view of sex: two people going hand-in-hand into the sunset, to do something, although it was not clear what. It was the man's job to make it work, while women merely needed to be beautiful and warm. This was quite shortlived. In the middle sixties we had a recreational view of sex – it was for fun, for pleasure, for having children at the point you wanted them. The only appreciable rise in birth rate is to women over thirty; therefore they are likely to have had some fifteen years of sexual involvement before they have a child. The liberation movement has something to do with this but it is not clear whether it is consequence or a cause. Women are freer, more independent, more demanding, more exciting, more all kinds of things.'

Paul Brown talked of the growth of 'orgasmic consciousness': 'The freedom of women to talk in terms of orgasms has helped them to conceptualize the misery of continual frustration. 'Abolishing frigidity has been an important achievement. It is now impossible to use the word in a professional way.' Nevertheless he admitted that the commonest problem presented by women was the inability to 'establish' orgasm ... ('don't lets say "achieve" it makes it sound like an examination') the problem of letting go, of responding to one's own body. Of course, the more relaxed one is the better ones does it; it is a question of confidence, of not having to prove anything.'

It was of course impossible to assess the incidence of this sort of difficulty – 'is it real or is it stimulated by study?' What Brown was certain of was that a lot of sexual misery can cause a lot of physiological discord and depression: 'A vast amount of depression is sexually based. But if you sweep round the other way you find that one third of gynaecological operations are unnecessary; doctors see patients with some kind of complaint and it's their job to cut it out.'

However, more women are willing to take control of their own sexuality: 'We are getting away from the ludicrous situation where a woman is asking the man "did I come" and the man never questioning whether he is the right person to be asked.

All of this alarms men and Paul Brown reckons that they are right to feel frightened at least for a while, until the balance of power sorts itself out. 'The harmful effects of the women's movement have been in the angry castrating, denials of the relevance of men. The good side is the "hey, we are people, recognize us" demand.'

Paul Brown thinks that in the 1980s marriage will go on, but that bad marriages will surface quicker: 'A significant shift is that the central concern in forming a marriage is "what is the quality of the relationship." Before it would have been "what is the economic security" and the roles would have been established on the basis of the men providing the security – to the extent where men would not allow women to work because it was his job to look after her. It is interesting that marriages now break up even in the face of considerable economic hardship, because one or other, or both, of the partners are not prepared to compromise on that. It was simple before: men were men and women were women; problems now are much more complex.'

Whether liberation has been a consequence or a cause of women's greater sexual freedom and information and improved standards of health care is, as Paul Brown noted, hard to disentangle. But beyond the dramatically obvious progress in women's well-being and education about themselves, the ancient taboos still lurk and ancient privileges are still afforded to the still higher earning male.

Modern mothers sigh with relief when their daughters marry

– not because they have unloaded an expensive liability, but because marriage somehow makes sexual activity (which probably long preceded the wedding night) 'safe'. Children are still 'protected' from sex although in that area education is improving too. And men are indulged, permitted their sex objects and their pecadillos and their coarse clubbable or pubbable jokes.

On the other hand 'getting a man' is so much a test of female worth *before* marriage, that it is scarcely surprising that after several years of living with the one she has caught, a woman gets to wondering again about her drawing and holding power.

'My husband's OK – we get along fine,' said one woman of forty. 'I don't know what I'd do if he ran off. I'd never get another man at my age. I'd miss out on sex – I've seen it happen to so many of my friends. I'd become a victim for men who thought I was so desperate for it that they were doing me a big favour by turning up on the doorstep with a bottle of booze and a silly smile on their face – all ready to comfort me in my erstwhile marriage bed.'

This woman who had previously worked in personnel management was also sceptical about what it would be like trying to earn an independent living:

'I know just what it would be like financially if I was on my own – even if I kept the house I wouldn't be able to keep it *up*. If I went back to work I'd have to go back to the bottom. I'd probably have to work part time because of the kids anyway. No thanks. My husband has his shortcomings but baby, it's cold outside.'

In spite of this apparent cynicism, the divorce rate rises. Paul Brown noted the unwillingness of partners to put up with an unsatisfactory sexual relationship. Some of this can be attributed to women's greater sexual experience and therefore greater awareness of alternatives. (The Office of Population Censuses and Surveys last year reported that more than half of all women are no longer virgins by their nineteenth birthday and that three-quarters of all brides have had sexual intercourse before marriage, against a third twenty years ago.)

But there is another side, and some people think that feminism has backfired a little here. As women have an increasingly competent and independent image, as they enjoy greater sexual freedom, but still marry according to the old rules, they place themselves in another, subtler sort of danger. Men are freed from the old fashioned sense of responsibility they were once asked to feel for the women they married and laid exclusive sexual claim to. Now they can with greater equanimity leave the wives who have grown middle aged alongside them, for a younger more liberated lady. In America middle-aged deserted wives with little or no equipment to survive alone in the world are called 'displaced homemakers' and special re-training centres are being established for them. Here their number is growing and their chances of a liberated and anything like self-fulfilled life are all too often slim.

Some feminists have seen the only solution to sexual inequity to be a complete turning away from men. Sisterhood is a friend-ship ideal, but it can have a sexual component. Woody Allen's joke 'My wife left me for another woman' is based in truth – and not just in Manhattan or some other psychiatrists' happy hunting ground. One wife said that the 'discovery that she was lesbian' had opened a whole new world to her, had made her understand what tenderness was for the first time since she married. On the other hand a leading feminist was impatient about the increasing lesbian element in the women's move-ment: 'Half of those women aren't *really* gay. It's just that they have cut themselves off from men to sit up all night licking envelopes with women. Naturally they become emotionally and then physically involved with each other just like prisoners do in single sex prisons.'

That is an apposite image – for any attempt to remove sex from its time honoured associations with bondage and property seems doomed in a country such as ours where all women under thirty questioned in the survey quoted above 'thought or hoped they would marry'. In the light of present statistics, ninety-five per cent of them will do so, 'at some time in their lives'.

Part Three

Some Realities

The women whose stories make up the next part of the book are in the main drawn from the age group – twenty-five to forty – most likely to have been affected by the changes of the last ten or fifteen years, and would have had some chance to hear the gospel of the women's movement.

They are only eight of them – a small selection from a much larger number of women interviewed – so there is no suggestion that they represent every aspect of housewifely life in this country.

Some have seen revolutions in their own lives – self created or otherwise. All of them are married and committed to the idea of sharing their lives with a man, and have to some extent worked out their own ways of solving difficulties presented in the age of liberation.

Lottie, now in her fifties, reminds us how radically the whole business of home-keeping has changed since the war; Abigail is a young doctor's wife starting out on the frighteningly lonesome but idealistic career of marriage and motherhood; June has given up dreams of accountancy for her baby and husband but rather hopes her daughter won't; Jane in Edinburgh hangs onto her un-expressed dreams while adjusting to running a home and family. Mary works hard to balance domestic perfection with striving towards an outside identity; Stephanie has abandoned a high-powered career to devote herself to home and husband. Margaret has found a way of getting out of the house and serving the community without cutting herself off from her children. Anna is one of the few women I have ever heard of who really has made the feminist ideal of equal sharing work – at some cost she admits.

E

Lottie: The Way We Were

I've always thought of myself as a housewife. You see, with the
war, those of us who were married couldn't wait to come home
safely so we could have a normal life. We wanted homes of our
own and children.

Lottie Griffiths and her husband Bill are true Londoners, born
and bred in Chelsea. They live in a three-storey, Victorian terraced house at World's End – the area at the bottom of the King's
Road. Lottie moved into the ground floor of the house during
the war, while Bill sat it out in Italian and German prison camps.

After he came home in 1945, having escaped from the
Germans and walked across half Europe before being picked up
by the Allied Forces, Bill worked as a window cleaner and then
as a taxi driver. Now he drives film stars around London in his
spanking new Mercedes.

Their house is a comfortable, family home. They bought it
from the landlord several years ago and it is constantly filled
with visitors and grandchildren. They have turned one of the
bedrooms into a luxurious bathroom and there are good pictures
on the walls and pieces of silver dotted about the living room, as
well as a grand collection of family photographs in one corner.
They are seriously considering letting the house and moving to
the country because, they say, London no longer belongs to
Londoners.

They have an exotic streak in their lives now. Bill often goes
away on location and takes Lottie with him so they might spend
three or four months of the year in Greece or Portugal while a
film is being made. Lottie has a scrapbook which includes
pictures of herself with Elliot Gould's arm round her shoulder.
But it wasn't always like that.

'I've been in this house since '43,' said Lottie. 'We got married in '42 after Bill went in the army, before he went away to fight. We were both nineteen. He went abroad about six months after we got married. He was in North Africa for about a month before he was captured and was a prisoner for the rest of the war.

'In the meantime I got this flat – I just had these two rooms and the kitchen. There were three families in the house altogether. Same in all the houses round here. We had one loo which we all used to share. Bill came home in '45 and Christine was born in September '46. Robert was born in 1950. With the two kids, we got rid of the big furniture and made this room into a bedroom as well as the other one, so we just used to sit in the kitchen with the wireless before we came into bed at night.

'When Bill came home I was still doing war work but Bill didn't know what to do because he was in the tiling trade before the war doing delicate mosaic work and it was the first thing everyone cut back on – that sort of luxury thing. So he didn't ever finish a trade. I was making tents and camouflage nets for the army. Bill decided to build up a window cleaning round then, while I was in hospital having our older son Robert, he got himself a permanent job with a window cleaning firm. He was rep with them and then a manager with his own depot and men under him. When Robert was about twelve, he took up the knowledge to be a taxi driver. He did that for about thirteen years until he went into the film industry, six years ago, as a driver.

'I've always worked, but I'm more or less the same as Bill. I went to a Catholic school where all they taught you was how to pray. My mum took me away from school before I was fourteen and got me a job looking after a little boy. I had no qualifications whatsoever. I didn't have any ambitions really, and I wasn't a very thinking person at that time. My family weren't talkers, we didn't have conversations. Bill was brought up in a house where he had about four uncles and he read books from tiny and they always had lots to talk about.

'I left that place when I turned fourteen and worked in a place that made slides for lantern slides, then I worked in a big central library which used to send books out to little shops. Little shops used to have lending libraries then; you could go into a little shop up the King's Road and, apart from selling sweets or cigarettes, they would lend books. Bill and I met when we were fifteen and went dating. Getting married in those days was a way of getting your own place and getting out of living with too many people in one room and several families in one house. Then the war came. I went into war work and then I tried to get out of that so I could join the forces but they wouldn't let you if you were doing war work. When the children were small I always had some sort of small job. When Christine was a baby in her pram I used to work for a doctor's wife – I did cleaning for about two hours a day and Christine sat outside in her pram.

'Things were very difficult after the war. Bill only brought home a few pounds a week. You could never make ends meet – you were always searching for an extra shilling at the end of the week. I used to mash up swedes and carrots for Christine and we always had semolina for sweet. You should see the pram Christine had! Even when Bill started with the window cleaning firm, he was only bringing home £6 a week and the rent on this place was 15/-. Everybody was in the same boat though. You never felt it was the end of the world if you had no money – you didn't lose sleep over it because you were young and it was – well – it was a way of life, not having any money.

'In those days you could stand in the street for hours and talk to everybody, but it's not like that now – now, everybody's too busy trying to keep up with the Joneses. In those days it was a very close community. Sometimes when you were talking to a neighbour, she'd happen to take out her purse, one of those concertina purses, and if you saw she had quite a bit of silver, you'd think, "Golly, she's got a lot of money!" When I look back on it, it was such a happy time. Having the children – you got so much pleasure from the children even though there was no money. When a baby was born, there were always lots and lots of presents because you could get something really nice for a few shillings. You always seemed to have clothes bought you. Families were very close. Both Bill and I saw at least one member of the family every day and we still do. They moved a lot of the family over to Battersea when they pulled down a lot of the streets round here to build the new World's End Estate, but I can tell you about lots of families where the brothers and sisters still see each other every day. When the mother and father die, the eldest child becomes the centre of the family and they go up to their house for their Sunday dinner.

'Things were hard for us but they were harder for my mother. My father was the youngest of fourteen and his sister Lillie married quite well. Her husband had a rag and bone shop in the King's Road by Chelsea Town Hall, and Mum used to go there and buy bits and pieces for me and cut them down to make me dresses. She used to buy bits of ribbons so I could have a bow round my neck to make me pretty. Her trade was a hand ironer in a laundry and she used to stand for hours pressing pleats into silk – they were never stitched in like they are now – and she used to do the same for my little dresses.

'I was born in a house behind Peter Jones, and of course we all lived in one room. It was quite a big double fronted house and there were three families in it. There was mum and dad and me and my brother, and there was another sister between me and my sister but she died of pneumonia when she was eighteen months old. There was one lavatory in the back for three families. My mum will be eighty in November and my father's father was ninety-four when he died.

'Housework then was so different from today. For instance, you had linoleum everywhere and if you had a rug, well, you were living in luxury and you put it by the bed so you had something warm to put your feet on in the morning. Every day you scrubbed the lino and then polished it with wax to keep it clean for the children. If you didn't have time to do it in the day, then you could still be doing it at 10.30 at night. The thing that really sticks in my mind was that I had nothing – only a cold water tap at the back so you had to boil up buckets and kettles to get hot water and then stand at the sink for at least two hours every day washing nappies after you'd boiled them in the bucket. We had an old tin bath for washing and when the children were little, we just used to sit them in the sink to wash them. Then you would have a pulley line out in the garden or on the balcony and you'd peg everything out. In the winter, your hands would be stiff with the cold and blue, and the washing would be stiff on the line. I didn't even have that Ascot out there until I had Gary (he was born in 1963). That was a big step forward, to turn on the tap and have hot water coming out. And then this washing machine – well, this washing machine, I sponge it down every time I use it and I stroke it. It's the best thing that ever happened to me this washing machine. I still stroke it. I've often said to Bill, if this washing machine pegs out I'm going out straight away to buy a new one. I couldn't live without it now. I did use the launderette down the King's Road. I used to think that was great, being able to load the pram and wheel it down there. The great thing about that was the driers – those enormous big driers for putting all wet things in. Even so, when it was snowing or icy, you'd still have to trot all the way down the King's Road with the pram. But an automatic washing machine is a miracle – you don't have to do anything.

'We used soda for washing dishes, to soften the water. God, it made your hands bad. Rubber gloves – you're joking, you couldn't afford rubber gloves. Your hands would be all cracked and in the winter, they'd bleed in the cold. For washing clothes, of course, you just used the big bars of Sunlight soap and scrubbed and scrubbed at the collars and cuffs. I had a big old porcelain sink but no draining board until Bill got someone to make me a wooden one and that was a real luxury, to have a draining board. Anything you wanted to get really white, like handkerchiefs, you'd boil it on the gas and the place would be full of steam! The condensation would be running down the walls.

'Look at it now – there's carpet everywhere; I just have to Hoover it. We had two coal fires and in the kitchen, we had an old range – it's still behind there and there's another one downstairs. We used to cook in the oven and use the top to boil kettles up on. The first thing you did when you got up in the morning was to clean out the grate and start chopping up the wood for the fire. If you couldn't afford coal, you went to the coke factory over in Fulham and you could get cheap coke from there to burn. In the winter, you'd have to get up that extra bit early in the morning to get the fire going before you brought the children down to dress them. My mum did the same thing. So did Bill's mum.

'Nowadays, I still get up to get Gary off to school. I make his breakfast and then Bill's, and get him off to work. I make packed lunch for Gary because his school doesn't do lunches. Then if

I'm going to do any washing, I fill up the washing machine, then I maybe come in here and stand and iron for about an hour and then I generally go through the house dusting and polishing and Hoovering and every now and then, just turning out a room. When I do a spring clean, I dust down the walls, clean the windows, wash and rehang the curtains and so on. But it's all so easy !

'I go through the house every day, not because I like to make work but because it's a dirty area. There's the power station just over the road so if you have the windows open all day, and the balcony door, there's a film of dirt everywhere by the evening. If you walked in here tomorrow and I hadn't dusted today you'd think this house was dirty. But then, some days I think, "I'll get out today" and I have my bath, get dressed and go out. Maybe look in the shops down the King's Road or go down to Peter Jones or go to Harrods and look at all the things I can't afford to buy. It's only this last eighteen months I haven't worked. Before that, I always worked, mostly cleaning jobs. I do look after two little boys once or twice a week which I adore. They're six and four and I find to be with children at that age so rewarding. I can remember when Robert was four – the conversations we used to have by the kitchen range with him sitting in his little chair. I can remember thinking I never wanted him to get older than four. At that age they live in a lovely fantasy world away from all the horrible adult problems. We have wonderful conversations, me and these little boys.

'The only thing I really regret in my life is not being educated properly. Now that the kids are gown up and even Gary will be off soon, it would be nice if I could shut the house up every day and go somewhere instead of going over it every day. I don't think the house is a trap exactly but if I had a nice job to go to it would take me out of myself. Now that I'm on my own a lot more, I really feel the need for company. I need to be stimulated by other people's conversation. I'm lucky that I'm married to somebody like Bill who talks a lot. I find that I'm just waiting for him to come home so I can ask him what he's done and who he's seen.

'There's only me and an old man in his eighties round the corner who are left out of all the people who were here when I moved in in '43. I've spoken to him ever since I've been here – they lived over the next garden. Lots of people have moved away because of their husband's jobs or family commitments or whatever. There were lots of people still left but then they made this an improvement area. The council bought lots of houses round here and now they've all got to be brought up to scratch so they've moved everyone into new flats in the area. They're given the option to move back once the houses are done but they like the new flats because they haven't had bathrooms and fitted kitchens before and they love it. Most of them are people whose children have grown up and gone away so a small flat is suitable for them anyway – why should they move back?

'We took over the top part of this house about twenty-five years ago when the family up there moved out. That was great because we could spread out of these three rooms and Christine and Robert could have rooms of their own. I've always thought of myself as a housewife. You see, with the war, those of us who were married *couldn't wait* for our men to come home safely so we could have a normal life – we wanted homes of our own, and children. Being a housewife was the ultimate goal. I always enjoyed work too, mind you. The girls I worked with through the war – well, we all had a very special kind of friend-ship because there was so much tragedy – you had to keep each other going. They were always coming in and they would have had a telegram from the War Office saying their husband or son or father was missing or captured or killed so we were very close – we helped each other. I missed it so much when the war ended and Bill was home but at the Pay Corps in the East End (they said he was too ill from being a prisoner to be discharged from the army so he worked in the East End for a while). When I stopped working after the war, I worked much harder at home than I ever had outside.

'I don't know if advertising influences me. Partly I suppose. I suppose I could well be but not so that I rush out and buy some-thing as soon as I see it advertised. I saw on television that you can get this marvellous spray which you spray on dirty collars and cuffs before you put shirts and things in the washing machine but I can't find it anywhere. I shop at the International at World's End and at Fine Fare in the King's Road and at Sains-

127

E*

burys. I try to do one big shop a week to get all my vegetables –
I can do more if Bill takes me in the car, otherwise I have to buy
what I can carry.

'My greatest pleasure is getting in the car and going out to the
country. We go to the cinema too and we love going to the
theatre. I just love getting out of the city. You look down all the
streets in this area and you'll see – there are absolutely no trees
anywhere. As soon as I get into the country I say to Bill, "Bill,
Bill, look at the trees!" They can't plant trees on the pavement
because there isn't anywhere for the roots to go.

'I love this house because I've been so happy here. Christine
was born in this room (now the living room). I used to go round
to a midwife near here and be examined by her but when it
came to having the baby, I had a terrible time. I was in labour
for almost two days. I was 7 stone 10lbs and the baby was nearly
9lbs and she was so long in the birth she was blue when she came
out. I had to be stitched up and in those days you didn't have
anything for the pain. My mum was holding my legs and it was
much worse than having the baby. Afterwards, I didn't get any
sleep because the young couple upstairs were always fighting
and screaming at each other. And on top of that I was breastfeeding but I had so much milk and Christine didn't take much
so my chest was enormous and as hard as a bullet. On the ninth
day after the birth I developed a fever and had to be rushed into
hospital. The doctor said to the students that women often get
ill from exhaustion after childbirth. I wouldn't recommend anyone to have children at home, certainly not the first one. I had
Robert in hospital and, even though it was only three years later,
they had this gas and air. Then they had this stronger stuff which
the Queen had when she had Prince Charles so that made it
alright. Of course when Gary was born I just had an injection to
be stitched up and didn't feel a thing.

'By then, Christine was seventeen and having a maternal instinct, like girls do, she helped me with the baby. She would
take him out for walks and things like that. He always used to
scream between his two o'clock and six o'clock feed and she
would bring him back from his walk screaming his head off. The
things I remember best about that period was Christine coming
home from work, Robert coming home from school, the baby

screaming and Bill coming in for his tea. I never knew whether to peel the potatoes or feed the baby. I was forty-one when I had him and I used to get so tired. I tried to breast feed him too, but he wouldn't take it very well and I always had gallons of milk. They used to express my milk and give it to the babies in the incubators. With the other two, the sister used to come round and express my milk by hand which was absolutely agony but with Gary they had a machine to do it.

'Bill has always helped me in the house. He would wash nappies and feed the babies. The only thing he didn't do was get up in the night, because he was such a heavy sleeper. I used to lean over him and pick up the baby, feed it and put it back without him stirring. If I was ill, though, something used to wake him up – he would always get up to the babies if I was ill. Even yesterday, before he went to meet his brother, he washed up all the breakfast things and then prepared all the vegetables for dinner. He always has been a marvellous husband. All he expects from me as a wife, is to be a loving wife. He likes us to tell each other everything and say we love each other every day. Bill has never expected me to skivvy for him. On the rare occasions that I've been out when he comes in, he makes his own tea and mine and has it ready. I used to get very run down when the children were small – partly because I fed them myself for so long, I think. So Bill would cook me meals and bring them up to me in bed and bathe and feed the children and put them to bed.

'What do I think of women's lib? – I don't. Don't agree with it at all. I think women lose a lot with all this women's lib. I'm very old-fashioned – I like to get on a bus and think a man will stand up for me if there aren't any seats left. That doesn't happen any more – women get shoved and pushed around and women don't get the respect that they used to have any more. Men don't doff their hats when they see a lady any more, do they? I agree with equal pay for equal work though – oh yes. You have to work so hard at domestic work and it's so underpaid. I think women are grossly underpaid in certain jobs. I can't think that I've been exploited though, because I've always been happy doing what I do. I've got good health and I'm happily married and I've got the best children in the world, so I feel every day is a great day, a new day. I think one day we'll move from here and get a little cottage in the country. I don't think that London belongs to Londoners any more. You always used to be so proud to be a Londoner when I went outside of the city but that feeling's gone.

'We complain a lot about not making enough money in this country, but when I think of the change in lifestyle since just after the war, when I first became a housewife – well, it's fantastic. I feel it especially when I go into young marrieds' houses – the things they have, it's absolutely unbelievable! Washing machines, fridges, tumble driers, deep freezes, dishwashers, Hoovers, and big gardens with lawns they've actually laid. The man just comes and puts down those turfs.

'When I think of these three rooms I got! My dad came and did them all up for me and I was delighted to have them. It was a big thing to have a place of your own for when your husband came back from the war. It was all furnished when he came back and of course he thought it was Buckingham Palace. And having children seems to be so easy now. Youngsters having babies go in the chemist every week and buy those throw away nappies – they don't go out and buy two dozen nappies like I used to. And they've got all these children's clothes that don't need to be ironed. They're all man made fibres so they just take them out of the tumble drier and fold them up and put them in the drawer. When I had the children, a lot of their clothes were pure silk and had to be ironed and ironed. And look at the irons. I used to have two irons which I put on the gas to heat them up and in the summer the heat was unbearable. You put a cloth on the table and did the ironing on that and in the summer, you'd have the front door open and the kitchen window open and the perspiration rolling off you.

'I'm sure young women are not any happier than I was standing at the kitchen sink doing all that work. Everybody seems to be so bored these days. We didn't have a television because Bill wouldn't have one and we used to play games all the time with the children or read to them or listen to stories on the wireless and get our pleasure like that. The greatest fun the children had was to sit up in bed after their baths and listen to Bill telling them stories of what it was like when he was a boy. All you hear about these days is youngsters having mental breakdowns and talking to psychiatrists. When I was young with the children, I didn't have time to think about myself. I remember one woman saying to me "Every time I think I'm going to have a nervous breakdown, I have another baby instead." Although I was never unhappy I sometimes used to get this urge to pick the kids up, put one under each arm and take off somewhere. It always happened in spring and I never knew where I might go, never. The biggest treat in those days if you had a few extra shillings was to get somebody in to look after the children and go to the pictures. Going to the pictures was a real treat.

'We were one of the first in the street to get an old banger to drive around in. Everybody used to say, "That Billie Griffiths, I knew he'd get on!" It was a Vauxhall and it was falling to pieces. On a Sunday, we'd fill the car up with people and go down to Brighton or somewhere else on the coast. We'd take a picnic and spread it out on the beach and the children would play. We'd sing all the way there and sing all the way back.'

Abigail: The Doctor's Wife

I am very dependent on David. Some people would say too much so. That hasn't changed since I had the baby; I just feel more vulnerable.

Abigail Hunt is twenty-five and has been married for almost four years; her baby daughter Francesca was four months old at the time of this interview. David, her husband, was a houseman at a big teaching hospital in the West Country. They met at Oxford and married immediately afterwards. Abigail has a 2:1 degree in English Literature and a Diploma in Education but chose to stay at home and do private tutoring rather than teach in a comprehensive school. She became pregnant shortly after finishing her diploma and continued teaching English to 'O' and 'A' level students and Oxbridge entrants until shortly before Francesca was born.

Abigail says she knows she is a housewife, but thinks there is something derogatory about the word and doesn't like to use it. 'I don't think I would ever put it on a form. I would leave the space blank. I wouldn't actually describe myself as a housewife. But I *feel* like one. Before I had Francesca, if someone asked me what I did, I said I was tutoring. Now I say "I've got a small baby, I look after her." To someone like you I might say that I felt like a real housewife this morning because I was Hoovering or doing the washing and to me, that's what housewives do. They wash the clothes, they get the husband's tea, they Hoover. That's what the word means to me and it's something I would hate to be. I was talking to someone the other day and saying that I'd turned into a real housewife and she said, "No, you're not a housewife. Housewives don't leave dirty dishes in the sink for days on end." I liked her for that.'

Hoovering apart, Abby doesn't much mind about appearances at home: 'I feel very embarrassed if the house is dirty, but I couldn't care less if it's untidy. Here, on wet days, we have to have the clothes horse inside with all the wet nappies on it and it depresses me. It makes me feel like a housewife. Now that I've got a baby, I have to do the washing every second day. That takes up the whole morning – well, two or three hours. I do a lot because she makes a lot of mess and I think it's important that it doesn't get so dusty that she starts sneezing. To me, dirt and untidiness are only important in their effect on health. It's not important to me as part of my image. My image is someone who collects a lot of clutter around them. Wherever we go we have plants and guinea pigs and posters and records. I need clutter, I collect it. David goes out of his mind. I can't bear to throw away letters or cards.

'This is a very institutional flat, I felt very concerned to make it ours. As soon as we arrived, we put posters up and we had the guinea pig in his cage and the candles and the rattles and the crib and fish mobiles flying around. We threw rugs over anything that was hospital property, and then I began to feel more comfortable. I like to have things around me because of the people they remind me of, not because of their material value. I don't like tatty things, mind you. I don't particularly care about money although I loathed being very poor when we couldn't have a bottle of wine occasionally and when we had to think before we asked anyone for the weekend because of the food they would eat. It got to the point where I had two pinafore dresses throughout my pregnancy, day in day out from four months onwards. I got very bored and very dowdy and I got fed up with the whole thing. That was a strain on us both, particularly with David's exams coming up. Although we don't live at a tremendous rate now, it's such luxury to have that bit extra.

'Before I had Francesca I used to Hoover throughout the house and do a big tidy every Sunday. I never washed the kitchen floor and I never ironed. I used to iron David's shirts for hospital but not anything else. I iron her stuff though. But I hate housework:

well, sometimes I don't mind it. I listen to the radio while I'm doing it because I think I ought to be getting something else out of it. I quite like shooting round with the Hoover. If the place really is dirty, it gives you a sense of satisfaction. But basically it's a bore and a waste of time and I don't care what people think of my home. The more gadgets that let me off doing housework the more I like it. I get no sense of satisfaction having lovingly scrubbed the kitchen floor if I don't think it needs it. There are some things I hate more than others and something I really loathe is ironing. That I resent doing. When I put the ironing board up, it feels to me like a scene out of *Look Back In Anger* – you know, Alison. Although David's not at all like that, I feel the aggression welling up in me and the resentment at the husband sitting in front of the television and the sound of the iron thumping down on the ironing board in the next room.

'When Francesca was first born David was fantastic. He certainly changed as many nappies as I did, and when we were both students, he did his share, far more than the average man. Now that he is a houseman, though, he works a hundred plus hours a week and when he does come in, I *couldn't* ask him to cook the supper or something. He can cook, though. When we first lived together he was hopeless. He only ever learned to do spaghetti bolognese or roast chicken. Then I completely took over the cooking but David still used to do the housework, often when I wouldn't. When I was pregnant, he used to do all the housework and the cooking because I couldn't stand the smell of food. He learnt everything although he used to ask me for instructions. I used to ask him to do the shopping when I was finding it very difficult to get out (I fainted all over the place right through pregnancy) but he could never look in the shops and see what was a good buy. He had to be told just what to get – 1 lb of fish, a 3 lb bit of lamb or whatever. That rather amused me.'

Abby hadn't thought of anything like 'household administration' as being part of her role, but felt that she knew more about it than David because she shops every day: 'I know all the different cuts, and how I'm going to cook them. I suppose I feel that he's not very sure of himself. From his point of view, he's buying the shopping for me, he's not buying it for supper. It's a two stage thing as far as he's concerned whereas obviously I don't see it like that. I know that he feels he ought to do more. He's not the sort of man who thinks that changing nappies damages his masculinity.

'I do a lot of my shopping in Sainsburys and I buy their brand of stuff. I always go for the cheapest. I don't buy everything at a supermarket. I go to the butcher's for meat, the grocer's for the vegetables, and the supermarket for washing up liquid and so on. Sometimes I see something on television and I think, "ooh, I'll try that." In Oxford, we used to get coupons through the door. I love those because it makes me feel as if I'm getting a present.'

The baby has meant that Abby has stopped earning her own money. 'Until now, I have always had my grant or tutoring money, and it was one of the things that I thought about very carefully. I always knew that I would hate to be given housekeeping. That whole thing really turns me off. We're in the middle of negotiating our joint bank accounts but it seems to be taking a long time for it all to get through. If I were buying something for myself, I would discuss it with David because it will be an account belonging as much to him as to me. And if he wanted something, I know he would discuss it with me. We always decide together what we can afford. Money is very much a joint thing with us. Even before we were married, I used to give David cheques if he went into the red. In those days, I was determined not to be financially beholden to him to the extent that I would give him the money for my half of lager rather than let him buy it for me.'

She would not, though, ever go up to the bar to buy the drinks herself. 'I am very dependent on David. Some people would say far too much. That hasn't changed since I had the baby; I just feel more vulnerable. I do sometimes go into a cold sweat when I hear of some man with a wife and two children who goes off and is never heard of again. I do want his support.'

Abby is extremely pretty and lively, but lack of money and an isolated life, mean she doesn't bother much with her appearance : 'I will certainly do far more for Francesca than I ever would for us. I wash her clothes separately and keep them separately and the only time I'm ever tidy is with her things. My mother said to me when she was down, that I must not fall into the trap that she fell into of thinking, "David needs a new shirt, he's at work all day. Nobody sees me so it doesn't matter what I look like" and letting myself get dowdier and dowdier. I think that has happened without me really noticing it. I usually look fairly scruffy anyway so I don't really mind. When she said that, though, it made me go out and get some material and make myself something that I really wanted. I suppose I'm the last, mind you. David's got the job, he has to look presentable.

The Hunts' day is a long one: 'we have a thermos flask beside my bed. The alarm goes at about 7.15 (this is if David's not being bleeped all night), Francesca is usually awake by this time and talking to herself, getting ready to demand food. We have coffee and feed her, and then I put her back in her crib where she talks to herself some more, or maybe goes back to sleep. Then David gets me my breakfast then goes to work. Then I have a bath while she's still in the crib. Then if it's a washing day I do the washing. By this time Francesca has had enough of the crib and I put her in her rocking cradle or she lies on her back on the rug. Sometimes I go and have coffee with one of the other hospital wives for an hour or so – Francesca enjoys that. It breaks up the day. I enjoy getting out and talking to another adult because often I do spend a whole day talking to nobody except Francesca and maybe one or two people in the shops. Last time I went to coffee with one of the wives I ended up spending twenty minutes talking about the advantages of the twin tub over the automatic. I came back here and thought, "My God, this is really not me." Anyway, then we have lunch; sometimes David nips around this time but not usually. Then we go out and shop and get the supper. Even if I don't have to get shopping, I usually take her out because we bump into people and they admire her and one chats a bit and perhaps we go round a park. It gets you out a bit. All the time, she's having feeds, don't forget. By that time, it's evening, David usually comes home for supper. Sounds awfully boring, doesn't it! If David is "on take", he won't come home. That happens every fourth night, but most nights he's back by seven. I try to plan to eat at about eight but often it's nearer nine. We have the evening together, but if he's been on take, and especially at the weekend, he doesn't come in till four in the morning and then he doesn't want to talk to me, he wants to go to sleep, wake up and have his supper and then go back to sleep. It's very frustrating. You've waited all weekend to talk to him, then there's really not much to say except to report on Francesca's teething. I do hate that bit of being a housewife.'

Motherhood, and the move from Oxford where they had many friends has left Abby very lonely: 'When we first arrived and we didn't know anybody I did feel very lonely and David wasn't around much. When we were students he was always there, much more than most husbands or boyfriends are. As students, we often worked in the same library. There was never a set time when he wasn't there. Even when we weren't under-graduates any more, we just carried on as if nothing had changed. Even while David was working at the Radcliffe just before his finals, he was in and out all the time. Getting married didn't really change anything, it just became more respectable. In Oxford I wouldn't have the same sense of feeling, "I am a housewife, doing her Hoovering." In Oxford, because I was there before we were married, I feel much more like just me and I go and see friends and all the housewifely duties are incorporated into doing other things. They don't become the main activities of the day. Here, the shopping or the Hoovering are often the main activities of the day.

'But this is actually the very first period of our time together that we've had a place to ourselves. We've always either shared with other people, or had lodgers. Even while David was away on locum, there was always someone in the house to talk to. In some ways I rather like being on our own. You needn't bother about putting dressing-gowns on when you go to the loo and so on, but in another way I do miss adult company. Anyway, I feel I can cope. I think I'm lucky because Francesca is relatively good now. But I understood about baby battering after I had her. I had imagined only ogres did it before. When she used to cry endlessly and I fed her and I changed her nappy and did all the things that the books say to do and still she cried I used to go almost mad. There we would be sitting up in bed at four o'clock in the morn-ing and then I really did feel desperate.

'Reading is one of the things I find I keep meaning to do. For the first time in my life I haven't really got a book on the go. I manage to get the Sunday papers read, but until I had Francesca I would read two or three novels a week. I was endlessly reading. I can't really concentrate on a book now. I could probably manage an Agatha Christie or two but if you are reading a book that is really taking your attention, it's awful if you have to keep stopping to do a feed or whatever. Even if I try to do something simple like putting up a hem, if she cries then, I find myself resenting it. It's because I can't concentrate on anything just for me.'

Television and radio provides company of a kind: 'We've never had a television until now, which makes a tremendous difference. I love the ads. If we turn to ITV, it's because I want to see the adverts. I find the whole thing very amusing. I've never been interested in women's magazines so I never buy them. If David's on take, I watch from eight until about twelve, if there's a good film on. If he's at home we often watch together. I listen to the wireless a lot, Radio 4, mainly. Sometimes Radio 3. I love *Woman's Hour*. I love plays because I can listen to them while I'm doing the housework. We listen to the gramophone less than we did before we had the television but there are so many evenings when there's nothing worth watching on television so we still listen to records quite a bit.

'When Francesca was first born and my mother was down, she used to babysit and I went to the pub once or twice with David just for half an hour and I loved that. It made me feel it was a link with the time before. It's such a tremendous upheaval having a baby, the life before and after are so very different and I do enjoy doing the sort of things that we did before. We can't go to films or theatres yet because she simply doesn't sleep for long enough stretches so that's something for the future. We've been able to take her with us to a lot of things – parties and weddings. She stays up for a while and then goes to sleep upstairs. It means we can be normal people and not just mummies and daddies, for a while. I find now that going on outings means a lot to me. I even enjoy our Sunday walks when we go to a green and watch a cricket match or something. I feel very grateful for it because it's a break from the routine. I do find the routine really tedious and depressing. I can quite understand why women feel resentful towards their husbands and their children and just everything. But I do think it makes a tremendous difference that I was older when I got married and older still when I had Francesca. I had done a lot of the things that you do when you're free. By the time she was born, I was fed up with going to the pub every evening.'

Abby seemed surprised that many people would think twenty-four was young to have a baby: 'I *felt* very old. In the ward, I was the second oldest. The only person older than me was a woman having her fourth baby. I was twenty-two when we got married which seemed quite old to me.

'I wouldn't say I was a feminist, although I like the best of all worlds. There's a girl who's pregnant at the moment; she's terribly keen to have a boy because she likes the idea of buying Meccano and Action Man (or her husband probably does), and it annoys me that she feels she could never introduce those kinds of toys to a daughter. I would fight for equal pay, for nurseries, for the right of women to choose their own way of life. I have chosen to stay at home but I feel very strongly that women should be able to go out to work if they need to and feel confident that their babies are being properly cared for. I would never have an abortion but I would fight for somebody else's right to have one. I suppose in my own way of life I'm not very liberated. I don't think I really need to be. Before I had the baby, I was just me, Abby. I wasn't "wife" or "girlfriend". I think that's one of the things that really strikes home now that I've got Francesca; I have become Dr Hunt's wife rather than just me. Not that I ever was a journalist, or a lawyer or anything, but I was just me. Now people say to me, "What does your husband do?". I would never say, "I'm a doctor's wife" but I do say, "I look after my baby" so I am really choosing the role of mother.

'I was terribly against the whole idea of getting married. When I was in my teens, I didn't think I'd marry and I certainly didn't think I'd have children. I didn't like the idea of the whole process. If anyone had told me five years ago that I would be sitting here, a wife and a mother, while my friends are successful career women, I wouldn't have believed them. But I'm very happy. I feel a bit of a cop out at times. I often wonder what I'd be doing now if Francesca hadn't come along, even though she wasn't exactly planned. I know I would have wanted to do a

B.Lit. That's the only big regret I have. I would have said, up until the time she appeared, that I would do it. Now, realistically, I don't know that I'll ever get round to it. I hope I do. It depends how it fits in with David now. It depends on where he gets his jobs; I've got to play second fiddle really. And also it depends on what sort of child Francesca turns out to be and how many others we have. It's not something I would ever want to exclude. When you get to be twenty-five – well, it's the old cliché; when you're very young you think you can do anything, be anything but at twenty-five you suddenly realize you're not going to do all these things – you're not going to be the next Virginia Woolf. I can remember my brother-in-law saying to me, the first time he saw me with Francesca, "Do you remember once saying that being like Virginia Woolf, spiteful, unhappy and finally committing suicide, but producing wonderful novels, was far better than having a baby and leading the sort of life you're leading now." And quite honestly, I do still feel like that – I do think that Virginia Woolf with all the heights and depths, is worth six million of me. But I don't have that kind of talent and I am very happy as I am although I do despise myself sometimes for being so content with the way things are. I laugh at myself a lot.

'I think the more you analyse it, the better it gets. And also, you think beyond just the role, to thinking that you've brought a baby into the world who might grow up and produce all these novels that you're never going to write. But that's not funny, it's something you've got to be very careful about – not to allow unfulfilled desires to become ambitions for your child. I get very emotional with Francesca in a way that I never thought I would. I don't think I'm a very maternal person – not at all – though I know some people see me as maternal. I have a picture of maternity that is not me. When I sat through Holocaust on television, I looked at her and thought, in all its triteness, that baby doesn't know anything about prejudice and hatred and cruelty. I thought, I can't bear her to grow up and know about them. When I hear on the news about terrorism and other sorts of violence, I think, what sort of world have I brought her into. Although having a baby has restricted me intellectually in some ways, in others it has stretched my mind because I think far more about my environment and what is going on around me. It matters more now.

'I can't say I particularly like the thought of pregnancy again, but I would do it for her. I don't want her to be an only child. I think an only child is more than just a child without brothers and sisters. There's something different about them. It's even more of a responsibility when there is only one, and I think if you have more, it shares the amount of responsibility the child eventually feels. I was rather frightened during pregnancy because I didn't really like children. I always used to think about Virginia Woolf's comment, "I love children. I particularly like other people's children because when they cry, someone comes and takes them away." I think that's brilliant and I was like that. I enjoyed other people's children for half an hour but no longer. So I really got quite frightened as I got fatter and fatter and the kicks started and I kept thinking, "But, will I be able to love it? Babies just lie there and they crap in their nappies and they puke up their milk and you have to clean up after them. For the first few weeks, they don't even smile." I thought I would probably quite like it after it was able to talk, but I didn't think I'd ever love it as much as I love her. The whole thing is very different from what I expected.

'I feel very much as I did at sixteen or seventeen. The veneer of being a wife and a mother is still something that's not really quite me. I *am* a wife, I *am* a mother but I don't think of myself as that any more than I really think of myself as a housewife. I think of it all as slightly absurd and I certainly think taking yourself very seriously as a wife and mother is a mistake. Often I think I've borrowed Francesca for the day. She's a pretty little doll; not exactly an animated doll because it's much more serious than that but I dress her up and put her in her sun bonnet and I suppose in that sense it can be a bit of a game.'

Shortly after this interview, Abigail and David returned to live in Oxford where Abigail felt she would be more at home and in close touch with old friends. She found, in fact, that she missed the new friends she had made and her sense of isolation increased because the house in Oxford is too far from the hospital for David to get home at night when he is on 'call'. Consequently, he is often away from home for days on end which Abigail finds difficult to cope with. They are considering selling the house and moving into a flat nearer the hospital so they can be more together.

June: Swings and Roundabouts

I've changed quite a lot since I got married and had her. I'm ever so quiet now. I used to be quite loud-mouthed. I feel less of a person I think because I don't feel I do anything.

June Dixon is a tall, clear-eyed, outspoken but jokey woman of twenty-seven who lives in a pre war block of council flats in South London with her mum, her husband Terry, and her three year old daughter Lucy.

'I've lived in this block all my life. My Dad was the caretaker so we used to live in the caretaker's flat. Then when he died they gave us this one. It's my mum's really.

'Terry and me met on this hill, when I was walking home one night. Him and his friend stopped and asked if I wanted a lift and I said no because I was already home. They asked me out so I said yes. I think they thought I would bring along a friend and were amazed when I turned up on my own to go out with both of them. Terry and I started seeing each other, on and off after that for about six months before we really started going steady. How am I going to tell my daughter that her father picked me up!?'

June divides her time between looking after Lucy and the flat and helping Terry at work (he strips pine furniture). 'Before I gave up work to have Lucy I was a PA with Cambridge University Press in the accounts department. I started as an accounts clerk but I was really fed up after the first week so they offered me the other job and I stayed for three years. I don't think I would have stayed any longer whether I'd been pregnant or not because I couldn't go anywhere. I would have had to take more exams. I might do that. Take some accountancy exams. I enjoy doing all my brother's books for the shop – and Terry's. It stops me from going stale. I shall probably start doing something about it in a year or so. It depends on how Terry's work goes and if he needs me to help him because if so, I wouldn't have time. I enjoy helping him; I like work.

'I get up about nine – sometimes later. We get Lucy up and she just runs around and amuses herself. Then we have breakfast. Monday I do the washing at the laundry here which takes up most of the morning. We don't go visiting on Mondays. I do some shopping in Forest Hill on Monday afternoons. In the winter we watch TV in the day but when it's warmer, we spend most of the day in the park across the road. If we're in, I do something about lunch for the kids but if we're out we get something for them. I never eat lunch. We often go and look in the shops in the afternoon. If we go to Peckham we spend four or five hours there because my brother's got an antique shop there. The kids love the shop. Then we come home and I cook. Terry comes home about half six but I usually eat with Lucy and my mother before he gets in. She usually goes to bed at seven and then we either go out, or stay in and watch telly. We're very lucky living with my mother because we can go out when we like and she babysits.'

Whatever she says June has a routine of sorts : 'I do the front room every day, and the bedrooms about once a week. I dust and Hoover and change the sheets – I change her bedclothes twice a week. I spend most of my time picking up toys and moving them from one place to another – or mending them. Most of the furniture belongs to my mother. I bought the cooker and some of the carpets. We usually go halves on everything. Ours and Lucy's bedroom furniture is ours. We spilt all the bills too.

'We're a close family. I'm never on my own and I can go out when I want. I've worked a bit since I had her, and when the firm I worked for moved to Cambridge I used to go up there for parties. My sister will always have her, or my mum.

'I don't think husbands and wives should work together but Terry was let down by a bloke who was going to start working for him this week. I don't think he can take working on his own much longer so rather than let the business down, I am going to help him. We get on alright working together because he doesn't boss me around – he isn't the type. I'm bossier than he is. I think we get on better than most couples would working together.

'I don't really think of myself as a housewife because I'm rarely indoors; I'm always going out visiting friends. We've got friends who live miles away so we go visiting two or three times a week for the day – me and Lucy and my sister and her little boy, Wesley. My sister comes over every day; she gets a bit bored on her own because she doesn't know many people where she lives.

'Well, maybe I am a housewife, but not a typical one. I know some typical ones and they get up at a certain time in the morning and make the breakfast and do the cleaning and the washing and cook the tea. It's all routine; I don't have a routine – I do all the housework at night for one thing. My mum works so you could say that I run the house; she cooks weekends but I do the rest.

'Terry expects the place to be tidy. If he comes home and I've had a hard day with her, because she can play up sometimes, and I don't feel like making him a cup of tea, he gets annoyed because he thinks it's my duty to do that sort of thing. I don't think it's my duty. I think I've had a harder day than him but they don't see it. I think housewives have a harder time at home than people who go out to work. Yesterday, I was working with Terry and when I got home at 6.30 I felt full of life, wanted to go out.

'Terry helps me with things when we're on our own together but not when my mum's here. When she's on holiday he helps with the cooking and cleaning and he makes a good cup of tea. I remember the first time he did the washing up – I couldn't believe it. He won't change nappies. He got used to feeding her after a couple of goes. To tell you the truth, I think he was terrified to touch her. I wouldn't let him get up to her in the night because he's one of these people who really needs his sleep and I could rest during the day.

'We've got a funny relationship; we're like brother and sister. People who don't know us often think we're brother and sister. I can't describe our relationship, really. We really get on, we never argue. We're mates really. We still feel romantic about each other – he loves going out, just the two of us for meals.

'I love cooking. I like trying out new things but Terry isn't a great one for my experiments! He likes conventional food; we have joints during the week because he won't eat stews and casseroles. I think he had a lot of them when he was a kid. It's a nuisance because casseroles are the sort of things I could prepare in the morning and then not have to worry about food when he comes in.

'I think I am influenced by advertising. If I see something new, I always try it. That's with food. With washing powders and things like that, I normally buy the cheapest. When she was a baby I bought the dearest to make her clothes soft. I think it's up to the individual. It wouldn't matter how good the ads were, they wouldn't persuade me to buy Stork margarine because I hate margarine. I buy my meat from the butcher's and my vegetables from the greengrocer's so I don't do all that much shopping in the supermarket. A van comes round the estate on Saturday so I can get bags of potatoes from it instead of carrying them home. Terry and I go to Shoppers Paradise in Penge once a month to buy all the tins. He likes corn and butter beans and peas occasionally. Lucy likes tinned tomatoes and you can get washing powder there and jars of jam and marmalade.

'This flat isn't the way we want it. Kids are so messy when they're young. We don't really intend to stay here but if we're still here in two years time we'll get a new three-piece and carpets. I can't stand the table in here or the three-piece – this room is nothing like I want it. I'd like a chesterfield suite covered in Dralon and shag pile carpets. I'd like a beige carpet and brown suite. I like pine in the kitchen but I wouldn't have it in the front room. I don't really like antiques. When Terry first started stripping pine furniture I used to think, "How can people have that stuff in their houses?" I've got used to it now because I worked in my brother's shop last summer and you have to try to like stuff if you're going to sell it. We have to have this place as it is because we're not allowed to knock any walls down. We really want to get a place of our own, which we can convert into two separate living quarters, one for us and one for my mum; that way we can have the mortgage in Terry's name but she'll pay her half towards it.

'Terry gets on really well with my mum otherwise it just wouldn't work. We live together as one big family. We couldn't live with Terry's mum – he couldn't live with her. I don't know how I'd get on if I couldn't live with my mum.

'I make most of the decisions. I don't usually ask anybody – I just go ahead and do things. If we need something I get it and he pays for it. Terry hates money so he gives it all to me and then if he wants anything, he takes what he needs. I've got a bank account and Terry's got a work one. We've got a joint building society account and we're managing to save a bit now; we couldn't before with some of the jobs Terry had, because the wages were low. He didn't train to do anything, that's the trouble. It's his own fault. He started off in the print but he was earning far less money than all his mates on building sites so he left. I think he regrets it now.

'If the business goes well, I will probably go on working for Terry but if the whole thing folds, I'm going to have to get a job again. I want to be an accountant but I don't think I'll ever get that far. I took A levels but I didn't get them because of my nerves. I did all the work and I was on tablets from the doctor for a week before but they didn't work. I took nine O levels and got six.

'We play badminton in our spare time and go swimming. I like going drinking best of all but Terry isn't too keen. I'm taking driving lessons too. I'd like to be able to drive so that I don't waste so much time getting to and from places by public transport.

'Just going shopping is such a hassle with kids. We've got some lovely parks around here but I'd like to be able to take her further – up to London sometimes.

'I've changed quite a lot since I got married and had her. I'm ever so quiet now. I used to be quite loud-mouthed. I feel less of a person, I think, because I don't feel I do anything. I was having this conversation with a friend last week and I was saying that I would have to buck myself up or I would just slide and slide. I could stay in all day, in my dressing-gown and not bother tidying up. When I worked I used to spend half my wages on clothes but I've only bought a couple of skirts since Christmas. I always wear make up because otherwise I spend all day telling people I'm not ill.

'I don't want to give the impression that I have to dominate Terry. It's not like that at all but he does like me taking the responsibility for most things. He hates money. I love it; the more the better as far as I'm concerned. He's not ambitious – I wish he was. He's beginning to slack just now which is why I feel I must go and help him. We've put a lot of money into that business so I shall be very upset if we don't get anything out of it.

'I don't think a lot of women's lib, but on the other hand, I don't think the woman's place is in the home. It's up to the individual. Every woman is different and I think these women's libbers think we all want the same thing. At the moment, I see myself as a part-time housewife, part-time worker. Full time work would be impossible for me with Lucy but when she goes to school things may change. I think firms should provide a crèche, then you can spend lunch-time with them. Most firms are big enough to set aside one room. It's the ideal solution for women on their own. A couple of my friends are alone with kids and trying to work. They had ideal husbands too. They never had to ask for anything.

'Terry is ideal for me but I don't think he would be for everyone. He's very laid back about everything. Not very get up and go. He lets things go by; he doesn't put himself out. He does as far as his family is concerned but not for himself. I know he does a dirty job but I think he could go to work looking less scruffy in the first place. I suppose I think too much about clothes and how people look. Terry isn't like that so I should accept that.

'I am happy but I want more. I don't think I'd be normal if I didn't want more. I expect if I had everything I'd still want more. I want a house; I really want a house. I want to make something of myself because when she leaves I'm not going to be that old and I don't want to just go and work in a shop. My sister has no ambition at all and I can't see the point in that. She can't see the point in being ambitious mind you. Even if Terry made a lot of money, I think I'd still want to do something, be somebody. I didn't enjoy work that much when I was there, and when I went back recently for a few weeks, I felt really insecure. I couldn't talk to anyone. I sat there for a week with my mouth shut. I started talking to this coloured girl and we made friends. I was very prejudiced but I'm not now so I suppose I learned something. We used to go to lunch and have a good chat, yet I couldn't talk to all the people I'd knew for years. When they started talking to me, I couldn't talk back to them so they stopped trying. That's when I thought I had really better do something. It's a terrible feeling. I was going to get a part-time job but I keep making appointments for interviews and not turning up because I get so nervous.

'Lucy was planned. Terry was desperate for a child. I didn't want one at all at the time. We had the choice of a baby or a mortgage which we could have got then because I was still working but we decided to have the baby. I don't regret it though – she's really worth it. I do regret that we had the big wedding instead of a house because we had a choice then too. I wanted the nice wedding. I thought, you only do it once, so I want the lot, and I had to pay for it myself because mum couldn't afford it. I didn't really enjoy it so it was a bit of a waste of money. I'm Catholic as well which had a lot to do with it. I have cut down going just now because she is so awful in church; I can't leave her with Terry because she has got to get used to going because she's being brought up a Catholic.'

June said that Terry wanted another baby and so did she because she wants Lucy to have a brother or sister but not yet, not until they get a bigger place. 'I can't see Lucy sharing her room with another baby. If I don't have another one before I'm thirty I shan't have one at all. I didn't have such an easy time with the first so I doubt a second would be any easier. I was pregnant during the hot summer and I had very high blood pressure. I had to stay in bed for a month before she was due, and then they took me in ahead of time and I had to stay in bed in hospital. Then they induced me and I had an epidural so I didn't feel anything. I'm still frightened of having a baby, because I missed all the natural childbirth bit. I had a lot of trouble with myself afterwards, too. I wish they'd waited instead of inducing me. Everyone I know has been induced.

'At home I put myself last. I think about Lucy and Terry and

149

my mum and then about myself. I suppose I think about mum more than anyone because she's on her own. I suppose Terry's my second baby. I've always taken charge. I probably married him partly because I knew he wouldn't boss me around and tell me what to do. I don't like being told what to do.'

She admits to being 'terribly possessive' about her daughter. 'I hope Lucy will do a lot with her life and her career. I hope she doesn't get married at sixteen and get pregnant.'

Jane: Growing Up

A housewife is a woman who is married, who chooses to live with a particular man. Everything else involved in the role is secondary.

Jane Lewis is thirty-four. She lives with her husband Iain, an architect, and their four boys in a Georgian terraced house in Edinburgh. The atmosphere is middle-class comfortable, rather than grand or in any way pretentious.

Jane was educated at a girls' public school and trained as a secretary. She gave up work when she married, fourteen years ago. Her first child Andrew was born a year later followed by Robert, now eleven, and the twins, James and Oliver. There is a thirteen year age difference between husband and wife.

Jane's family background was affluent, indulgent. 'Well heeled' is how she describes it: 'My father was always dipping in his pocket, and I always got more than I needed.' But she looks to her parents' stern conservatism as one of the pillars of her marriage: she would have got short shrift from them if she had ever run home to mother.

She left school at sixteen because, as the youngest of four children, she was always trying to keep up with the others. 'My father got fed up with being pestered by me so I left. I was told I was university material and I greatly regret now that I didn't go to university – or at least do *something* instead of getting married so young. I planned to work my way round the world with a friend but my father said I couldn't go until I was qualified as something. I opted for secretarial because it was the easiest and quickest thing to do and I could use it wherever I went. At the time what I actually wanted to do was shoe design.

'After doing the secretarial course in London, I came back to

Scotland to spend a few months getting to know my parents because I hadn't been with them properly since I was nine. During that time I met my husband. Iain told me to go off for a year and travel and enjoy myself, but in those days a year seemed like a lifetime. So I got married when I was twenty and a year later I had Andrew.'

Jane does see herself as a housewife, but not a very efficient one, she says. To her the word means 'a woman who is married, who chooses to live with a particular man. Everything else involved in the role is secondary. The idea of marriage is to have a family and to bring up children, but basically being a housewife is living with and caring for and loving a man.'

So, Iain comes first. 'It was the same in my childhood. My mother made no bones about the fact that life revolved around my father and we came second. A very close second but second. It was father and his wishes first.'

Jane was not brought up to believe she was destined to be a housewife. Not in so many words, at any rate. 'I don't think I was conditioned in any way. It was hoped and sort of understood that all three daughters would marry. We were not pushed in that way, but it was felt that our parents' lives would be fulfilled if their daughters were all happily married.

'My parents have a very conventional marriage but my mother has always had somebody to clean the house for her. She basically did the cooking.'

In spite of her declared priorities, Jane is ambivalent, even contradictory about her housewifery. In public, at a party, she says she probably hides the domestic side of herself: 'I think that the average housewife that I meet is a little bit boring. I don't talk about that – it's private, it's my family. It is my life, but I try to talk about everything *except* the family because I think that is boring news to most people. I don't think I'd ever say I was a housewife – unless I'm talking to someone who is *so* career orientated that I say it just to be bloody minded. But I think that your average housewife is a bore to talk to.

'At home I see my prime duties to be loving, to provide plenty of warm, cosy food, and to make sure that there is always clean laundry ready to put on. I think that if you make sure of those things, the family will turn a blind eye to most of your shortcomings. As far as people who come through the door are concerned, they can take me as I am and if they don't like it I've got plenty of other friends.

'I rate myself personally very low. I have a very low opinion of myself really. I think in this household I am very important, although I don't particularly like myself. The children certainly get very anxious and worried if I'm not here when they come back from school and they get bothered, and so does Iain, if meals aren't ready and so on. I am dealing with five men, and they do like continuity, the fact that I'm always there. If I come back late and they've all been at home together, there's a definite agitated atmosphere in the house.'

Jane found it hard to explain frankly why she didn't like herself: 'Well, I do nice kind things and I put on this show of being a nice sort of person, but all the time these terrible, wicked things are going through my head (she wouldn't give details). I think most people think I am nice but I'm really not, you know.

'I've come to the conclusion that I have been cheating myself living in a society, in a city, where certain things are expected of you and you come up with them but that's not really how you want to be. You want to be wild as the wind and free as air. But there are certain codes of conduct to which you simply must adhere. If you care about the people round you, and have a sense of duty, then there will always be restrictions. It's naive to pretend they are not there but I do find them confining.

'As a wife and mother I am confined in certain ways but so is everybody. Everybody has certain boundaries and maturity is knowing them, accepting them and going on from there.'

Jane has her own way of organizing practical housework. 'I do nothing until it looks revolting. The bathroom and the kitchen are usually clean but that's about it. I haven't had any help for about four years. Mrs MacDonald (who used to clean for her and look after the twins for the odd morning) and I are still friends and the twins go round to see her, but she was told by the doctor not to go on working. I want help in the house but when you're paying £1 an hour you resent how little they do for it.

'I probably do about two-and-a-half hours of housework a week. It's a jumble this house, but it is quite a clean jumble and that's what is important – as long as there is enough space for people to sit. This (an upstairs drawing-room) is the most decent room; we had to jazz it up a bit for a meeting and it is basically out of bounds to the children. It's a bit like a doctor's waiting room; it hasn't got the kind of jumble in it that we're used to.'

The room is large with a high ceiling and a polished wood floor. The walls are painted a smart buff colour and on either side of the original Georgian fireplace is a comfortable three-seater sofa covered in pale pink satin and two large armchairs covered with creamy tweed. There are several modern prints on the walls, and down one side of the room, a stereo, a white portable television, some low white cupboard units and between the two windows, a clavichord which Iain plays.

Iain helps with the physical housework 'up to a point' says Jane. 'He would never get the ironing board out because it is not his province and has something to do with our age difference. But he baths the children and makes sure they do their teeth and that kind of thing. He doesn't do the washing up because Granny died and left a legacy and I bought a dishwasher.'

She does not expect more of him. 'He has a lot of stresses and strains at work and he is the major breadwinner. I don't think that it is reasonable for me to ask him. I do ask for help when I really need it and I find there is no reluctance. It's like money, you know, "just ask me, just ask me" but there are some things you are brought up to ask for and some you expect to be offered. I think it should be jolly well offered.

'I think the worst time for housewives is when you are totally bogged down by children. When you don't even have a whole morning free, you begin to lose your self-confidence, you begin to feel unattractive because there is this constant demand for food – constant crying and frustration – and that's when you start to bang your head against walls. That's when you need a very understanding man to say "I've fixed the babysitter, I've got the table booked and we're going out for the evening," or something. At that stage, I think a lot depends on the husband.

'Iain is very supportive now but he wasn't originally. He didn't understand, he was brought up in a totally different way and, as we had all boys, he thought it was not right that as their father he should love them and cuddle them and dandle them on

154

his knee. It wasn't until the twins that he realized that if the children came up and demanded physical affection, that it must be given. After the twins were born though, his attitude changed dramatically; he had sufficient confidence to let himself go after the second child.

'I'm the disciplinarian in the family because he's a creative, aesthetic sort of man who tends to say anything for the sake of peace. I think that's a lot to do with why the children are a bit unco-operative. I think that has mended itself now, but for a long time that niggled me. If you are trying to discipline kids and love them too, it's very difficult.

'I think that if you are going to bring up a happy well-adjusted young family, you must have a happy marriage. In this day and age when people don't really usually inherit property and money, the only vital ingredient is a well balanced family life and they can go on and make their own relationships. My parents would never fight in front of the children and I think that is wrong. Children should be allowed to hear the verbal fights and also the loving side of it and my children do see that.'

The house inevitably, jumble or not, reflects an architect's eye. But Jane's influence is growing. 'Up till a year ago, Iain was so involved in being an architect that he decided on everything and I thought he was ever so correct. But I discovered, not long ago, that he is absolutely terrified of colour. Everything was black, brown, white or beige. In the end I got absolutely sick of it. I put my foot down and the results were terrific. Robert was allowed to choose the colour of his own bedroom as long as he kept it tidy. He chose bright, bright green and our hearts sank but it has been remarkably successful, it's one of the nicest rooms in the house. We definitely consult each other about decorating but I am getting much bolder.

'No, I am not a materialist. I like the feel of good quality clothes and luxurious touches. I can admire them on other people but if I won the pools tomorrow the money wouldn't be blown on high living. I would buy a little house that I have always wanted on the West Coast of Scotland – I suppose that is materialistic – but I'm not interested in diamonds and furs.

'I don't take as much care of my appearance as I used to. I think I have grown beyond that or maybe it has grown beyond me but I really don't think that clothes are important. As long as you are clean and fresh and don't stink, I think that is all that is important. I think too many people place too much importance on what people look like, how their homes look. I have never in my life criticized someone's appearance or the look of their home.

'What money gives you is choice, that is the real miracle of money but I'm not craving for luxurious trappings. I had a very well heeled childhood, but by marrying Iain I got a completely different outlook on life – he made me look at trees and the branches and the patterns they make against the sky, and I feel so much richer than before I knew him – I feel completely involved in life. I must always have had another dimension waiting to be tapped but my upbringing certainly never brought it out. I think I was the most misunderstood of the children, but also the most ungiving.

'But of course I *have* resented being short of money, particularly when we were first married. But we're *still* short of money, all those years later and yet we've always managed to do the things we really wanted to do. We've certainly had fights about it and I've thrown in the odd dart about the sort of money I used to have, but came to realize it didn't really matter. You can have a lot of fun without money.

'We have two quite separate accounts in two quite different banking organizations. I had my own bank account when I married and I keep it that way because there is a certain amount of privacy which I like to maintain. My husband gets his pay cheque – I know what it is but I keep forgetting, but he's not reluctant to tell me. He gives me a certain amount every month which I put into my account but it's nowhere near what I spend. I started working part-time four years ago to have some pocket money that I could spend on presents and extras but that money has now become an absolute necessity – I really don't think we could live without it. The £125 (1978) he gives me is on monthly banker's order and he never asks me what I spend it on. Out of my money (including the £125) I buy all the things we need for the house except things like new shoes for the children. He pays for that kind of thing and all the electricity, gas and phone costs.'

Jane is actually doing several part-time jobs, a fact which she announces with evident glee. 'My basic money, which is below the married woman's allowance, so that I don't get taxed, comes from working for a food firm as a merchandizer which sounds very grand but is basically stocking supermarket shelves. It's quite lucrative because they don't pay by the hour, they pay by how much you put into the store that you're working in. You can really rev it up and if you work fast, you can get it done in half the time you're supposed to take.

'So I basically work five hours a week for £11 which is more than I used to get for secretarial work. I'm involved in various other things too – I'm trying to help my brother set up an import/export operation between here and Hong Kong. I'm trying to flog flowers for somebody because we're using their telex for the company. I try to set up deals with hotels and big business corporations. I'm still doing a bit of hotel reception work, and there I often end up chambermaiding and working in the bar if somebody's off sick. I don't mind what I do as long as I get paid for it.'

In spite of her supermarket activities, Jane says she is absolutely *not* influenced by advertising as a housewife. 'No way. When I go shopping I just buy what I need and sometimes I splurge on something the children are asking for because they're influenced by television – but I'm certainly not. I don't watch television really except sometimes on Sunday night.

'There are lots of things I like doing in my spare time but that time is absolutely governed by the family. I'm desperate to get on with my weaving which I haven't done for about a year and a half but the family gets in the way, unfortunately. Not that I really mind that. We tend to involve ourselves in lots of outdoor activities which don't cost a lot, like climbing, walking, fishing – just spending a lot of time in the countryside. I like reading but because I have so little time to myself, it has to be escapist stuff.

'My expectations of marriage were very flippant, very light-hearted. I would be the person my husband came home to every night with joy because there I'd be, waiting for him, beautifully dressed, perfect dinner on the stove and he'd love me to eternity. I'd pick flowers all day long and arrange them in vases and just wander about on cloud nine. It was unbelievable now that I look back on it – totally unrealistic. I got a hell of a shock but I think my husband probably got a bigger shock.' (Much mirth.) 'I'll never forget after about three or four months, expecting a baby and having to go out to a shop and buy a book to find out what on earth was happening to me.

'It's terribly sad when you think how little I had to bring into the marriage in the beginning – that kind of ignorance is pathetic. After the first six weeks, Iain was thinking, "What the hell have I married?". We went back to his bachelor flat after our honeymoon, in which at least one of the bachelors remained; he was completely insensitive to the way I felt about being so young, inhibited and newly married and I was expected to just play the role of the model wife. Until we got into our own home (which at that point was uninhabitable) it was just unbelievable. Iain remembers it all but strangely enough, I think I have obliterated the first two years of our marriage from my mind – it was so bloody hellish. He certainly remembers it – for a long stretch it was uppermost in his mind.

'When you are young you have great expectations of life. It's a totally selfish outlook you have at that time. As you get older you realize you are never going to attain all those goals – you have set yourself too high a standard. If you can only attain half of it, or a quarter of it and still be happy or just content, then you have achieved a mighty lot. Youth is Utopia. Without being bitter, you've got to realize it was foolish to dream these dreams really. That sounds sad but even if you achieve contentment and nothing else, then you've got an awful lot more than most people. I wanted to travel and meet people, and it will probably happen before the end of the day, but I no longer feel frantic about it.

'The whole basis of our marriage was that I had to grow up within it and I know that presented enormous problems to my already mature husband. We weathered the storm and it was me growing up that did it. I think the marriage could easily be finished now if I didn't have such strong, deeply conservative parents. Whenever I thought of packing my bags, I always thought, where shall I go because if I go home they'll send me right back and say, "Just get your back into it and work hard at it because you've got a good thing there." And it *is* worth working through. I've talked to so many people who say the same thing – work, work, work at it. Anything worth having is worth working for.

'We went through an extraordinary thing recently which Iain was very reluctant to have anything to do with but which I was asked to do by my church. It was a thing called a "Marriage Enrichment Course". Iain threw up his hands in horror at the whole idea. I managed to persuade him he had everything to gain and nothing to lose. He got an awful lot more out of it than I did because I had been through so much soul-searching already – trying to grow up and come to terms with life. I learnt several things about him which I now realize must have coloured those first two years of marriage. After the course, he realized that he hadn't come into marriage truthfully either. It was a tremendous revelation. He hadn't realized that he probably married me on the rebound. Every Wednesday evening for about twelve weeks, we used to come back here, just the two of us, and talk about fundamental things – caring and sharing and various kinds of immorality – what your marriage vows meant – about the children and parents and what a Christian way of life should be about. We talked about all sorts of things we haven't talked about for years and years.

'It was very interesting to re-examine all the views we had in our pre-marriage days and find that after fourteen years we really weren't very far apart on all the fundamental issues – extra commitments and the family could have caused us to move apart in certain ways but this hadn't happened. Iain is not normally a good communicator – he is pretty inhibited, but through this he gave a lot.'

She now has no complaints about her housewife role: 'No, I've come to terms with that, definitely. Speaking personally, and this is strictly personal, I think if you have children, there is a definite role, a definite commitment you have to make. A mum should be there when they come home from school – she doesn't have to do anything wonderful – just be there to talk to and show things to. I envy people who have a career but I don't think that's the right way to bring up children. It's only fifteen or sixteen years out of your life and I think you have a duty to your children to give them that much.

F *

'I definitely still want a career – there's no question about that. But not until the twins are about fifteen or sixteen. But I think I've got a lot to give and I want to get wrapped up in something – absorbed in something. I don't want to do something half-heartedly; the main thing is not to run before you can walk. I've lost a lot of self-confidence being at home all the time. I don't look down on women who want to be housewives forever and ever but that's not for me. Having thought about it, I can wait but there have been a lot of traumas. I just didn't realize that there are about seventy years to your life. I thought, it has to happen *now* but of course it doesn't. Once you've got over that, and realized that it will happen sometime if it's meant to, you get so much more satisfaction out of life as it is at that point. Ten years ago was a very bad time – kicking, fighting. Nobody understood me and I didn't understand anybody. I had two children then and I was fighting to get out but once I had reconciled myself to the way things were, I was alright.'

This enlightenment didn't happen until she was thirty years old. 'It was an instant thing – it just happened overnight. I was terribly coloured by a friend of mine's imminent divorce. She had told me that Iain wasn't doing the right thing by me, and I was terribly influenced by that. I decided that I didn't have a happy marriage, that everything had gone wrong. I went to see a clergyman whom I had always looked upon as a second father, and my doctor, who again was like a father. I discovered that my doctor was quite a sick man and that the clergyman too, was ill. He had a great lump on his jaw and was about to undergo surgery. He had a wife and four children and he was worried out of his mind. That is the night when I grew up.'

Mary: Chaos at Bay

> I had set up and perfected the house and then I found that it
> was so basically unsatisfactory that it was driving me crackers;
> I spent my life *wiping* it.

Mary Laughton is in her mid thirties and has been married for ten
years to James, an increasingly successful manager in industry.
They both grew up in Northern Ireland, where their respective
families were part of the commercial establishment, but they
now live in London. They did not actually meet until they were
both over twenty, although, in true provincial style, 'knew of'
each other from childhood. Thus a kind of tribal confidence is
still evident in their dealings with each other. Their marriage is
utterly 'appropriate'.

Although they have always 'had money', (Mary has her own
private income, albeit modest) and come from a society where
money not only talks but speaks volumes, they share a traditional Puritanism – the canny, even stern, anti-extravagant bias
of their ancestors.

Which is not to imply that they are ascetic or mean, or above
a delight in the good things of life. It is simply that their indul-
gences are selected with care. Good silver, good (but not too
many) clothes, good furniture, hard wearing excellence in all
things. At home, their style is discreetly affluent. They live in a
four-bedroomed, modern town house in north London, and talk
from time to time about moving to a large one in the country.
James has one grand passion, which is also his greatest self-
indulgence: a forty-foot yacht. It is kept on the south coast and
sailed by himself, Mary and their five-year-old son Sebastian
every weekend in the season.

161

Mary is a wonderful cook, and cares as much for the look of the table and the dish as for its savour. She hates waste and every aspect of any experience must be appreciated; nothing is glossed over. *Thoroughly* imaginative would be a good catch phrase for her.

James travels a good deal and is usually away from home for two, maybe three nights a week. When he is at home he likes peace, Match of the Day, reading what his wife calls good bad books, and simply being with his family.

Mary is academic by training and instinct, but, apart from a couple of teaching stints abroad, she has never had a straight-forward job, either before or after marriage.

Although she takes housework deeply seriously as a hedge against chaos, which she fears a great deal more than male op-pression, she spent many years agonizing about what other job she might do. Most employment available to a graduate, un-trained, and married, and over the age of thirty, is uninspiring and/or pays poorly. Mary eventually decided to return to the library, and is currently working on a biography for which she has found an eager publisher.

For ninety per cent of the week, Mary says, she and her hus-band are running in separate grooves so 'there are very few times that we have to confront each other and what we are.'

Mary quite confidently declared that she was the equal of her husband and then, laughing, decided that was too modest: she was superior, and vastly so. Seriously, though, she did think that each of them had equal value and importance within the mar-riage, as they balanced their roles.

'I think we should have equal opportunity. But I certainly allow him to shoulder the vast proportion of the financial burdens, so it's really very unfair of me to say that we are equal. I have opted out of a great deal. Circumstances have made it so that I have not done anything comparable to him in financial terms. That is one of my obsessions. I know that I could not hope to maintain the standard of life that I am living, if I were doing it alone. It is not just that I am doing work that is unpaid for now, it is simply that if I were the sole supporter of the family, our life would be quite different. If I were suddenly left alone, I would get a job perhaps at £3000 a year, teaching. I would be starting at the bottom, getting virtually nothing.'

She acknowledges James as a protection between herself, and her son, and a very tough existence. 'He is freedom. He is also sexual freedom, not just financial freedom. He has relieved me of the terrible worry of needing to attract, having to be successful in sexual terms, which is a great blessing to me. You can enjoy little flutterings on the side but you don't have to make it in any real sense. It's lovely.

'Being married, and at home, is a wonderful barrier between yourself and a whole lot of rather vexed questions. As long as you can manipulate the insides, the kernel of it, to your satisfaction, it's a very good place to be.

'I'm not talking about freedom in the musical-hall-joke sense of the married woman who stops caring about her appearance; in some ways I care more – that's age I suppose. It's just a nice little cave to have crawled into. It doesn't matter any more if I find myself with a whole lot of men who don't find me attractive ... well, they may do, but I'm not looking any more. I've laid the ghosts of the provincial dance floors. At seventeen I was by no means what was wanted by the youth of my home town.'

In spite of being stung by the real or imagined slights of adolescence, Mary Laughton says that she did not think of marriage as an ultimate necessity when she was growing up. 'In fact I didn't think about it at all; I honestly didn't think of getting married until I was asked.' She said 'no' to her first proposer, who she met abroad, and then went back to her roots and met James. 'In a sense he was a vindication of my background.'

She does admit that her post-graduate work (she has an M.Litt) was conducted with the feeling somewhere buried that it didn't really matter very much, and that she would eventually get married. 'I didn't think in *terms* of getting married; but then I didn't think in terms of very much. There seemed to be no particular pattern for me and I did my M.Litt for lack of anything better to do. I had no clear view of myself and of what my role should be. I was open to accident, and marriage is what happened.'

She recalls, on her wedding eve, shocking a friend by remarking that, of course, you are never related to your husband. She still enjoys the fact that she shares a history with her in-laws but says that the saving grace in her relationship with them is that she is *of* them, but not *one* of them.

To Mary, a house is a labour of love and loathing, and she is determined to get it right, not to let it defeat her. She has put together houses for her mother in the past and, since her marriage, has lived in a succession of homes both in London and abroad. Her present house is as near to perfect as it could be within her, and its own limits, although she has relaxed her domestic rigour a little over the years. She recalls with a blush now, how when they just moved in, she wouldn't invite any of her neighbours to dinner until she had got the place in order, even though she and James were repeatedly invited, and the putting-in-order took two years.

'It was awful of me . . . I'd never do that again. Now it rather worries me that the people in the street have this image of us as the wealthy young couple with yachts and company cars and so on. That displeases me.

'The house does mean a lot. But it meant more before I started work again. I just am very obsessive about domestic organization. James is always teasing me about the time I shouted, "quick, fetch a hot cloth" when he spilled something. "You've been polishing the toaster again," he's always saying. I can't settle until I know that my physical environment is ordered, but that is not necessarily a bad thing.

'Before I started this research I was in the situation where I had set up and perfected the house, and then I found that it was so basically unsatisfactory that it was driving me crackers and that I spent my life *wiping* it. I just had to start work outside of it, or at least irrelevant to it.

'I spent a long time deciding. I'm free of the necessity of earning, so I could do that. Also I wanted something that made sense in terms of James's salary (for tax reasons) and with having a child. I thought of going into business, I even had an interview for a job as someone's office manager. But I realized that it would make my life so similar to the one that James leads – I mean I would have just come home shaking and tremulous every night – that it was absurd.

'I considered training in speech therapy, but I could see that

I would have just been beaten down by the hierarchy. I'm an intellectually proud person, and I would have found that intolerable. Then a friend suggested the subject for this biography. Whether it finally works out or not, it has still be appropriate, working for myself without any external structure. The work is exciting and although it is also isolating and virtually unpaid, it offers a chance for self exploration and self education.'

Mary spends most mornings in the London library or the British Museum. Her son, whom she adores, went first to a nursery and playgroup and is now at school.

'James is entirely pleased about what I'm doing. He was very fed up with my agonizing over what I should do. He found it very hard to take seriously at first, because it is such an invisible and solitary occupation, although he now has the tangible proof of other people's opinions – contracts and so on. All the same, there is no way that I am not going to have to fulfil his domestic demands. Mind you I'm as hooked on them as he is. He likes an ordered house; I like it more. My work doesn't stop him asking me to do things which are quite incompatible with a regular working day. I no longer organize the car servicing; I've got rid of that. But all the accounts and correspondence and all the organization of the family is done by me, both paper and figure work.

'This "admin" takes about two or three hours a week in paper work, but it is never regular. All the usual female duties, such as buying a birthday card for his mother, take a great deal longer. Present buying, cards, social contacts, are instigated and sustained by me. And of course, all the cooking. James makes the coffee after dinner if the News doesn't come on first and he gallops upstairs. I don't have to wash the dishes though. I am well served by machines for all that sort of thing.'

James's job carries a predictable weight of hours and anxiety as well as constant travel. He is paid well for his trouble, but Mary doesn't really think the company takes her existence into account and she does not, as Selma James might (see pages 65–78) see herself as an ancilliary employee, servicing the efficiency of an important cog in their machinery, although that is part of what she does all the same.

'I think those huge companies think the function of wives is to remain absolutely invisible and undemanding. That's all. We have no role whatsoever. They just don't want to know – almost to the point where I think they would almost prefer to have single or divorced men in top jobs. They are less trouble, have no appendages. Of course it works both ways, in that I am not called upon to do anything at all, entertaining or anything, for them.'

Although James travels, he is rarely away for very long – ten days is the longest trip he has ever taken. He says that as a couple he and Mary accept this but they are unusual; most of the other wives are very intolerant of their husbands being away after 7 o'clock in the evening.

Time together at the end of the day means a lot to Mary too: 'When James comes home early, before Sebastian goes to bed, the evenings are very pleasant. Even the fact that we are both tired is nice. It is a mellow, undemanding time. And we get immense pleasure out of the weekends. Funnily enough, I love it when the three of us get into the car and we are together, alone, for two or three hours. I get great pleasure out of that that I don't get at any other time; all we want to do is enjoy Sebastian and enjoy one another.'

On board the boat, equality tends to evaporate. 'The minute he steps on board, he puts his admiral's hat on; he says somebody has to be in absolute charge. So sometimes in the car on the way home I am boiling with rage because he has been so impossible during the weekend. Or I have had to do too much cooking. In the winter on Sunday mornings we lounge about at home reading the paper while Sebastian plays. That's delightful.'

Mary has no doubt that she is the lynch pin, the absolutely essential centre of their whole existence. 'I'm the one who gets things moving and organized. At the weekend (the boat apart) we are all in my world, the domestic one. I rule the house. I decide where everything goes and how everything should look. If you ask me where anything is in the house, I can tell you down to the last inch in each cupboard. This is my role. Every so often I say, goddamit why doesn't he do this, that or the other. On the other hand, I would be very loath to give up my control. I am *jealous* of my control of the system. Just as, if I went into his office and moved all his pencils out of one drawer and his paper out of another, he would hit the roof.

'I would not complain about what is usually called house-work. Once you've organized a house to this level everything is much easier – careful storage, a system of food and so on. If someone moved in for a week to run the house, I could give them a blueprint of what happened. Perhaps I'm being unjust, but I feel that if I left James here alone for several days chaos would break loose. I am haunted by chaos; to me it is alive wait-ing to swallow us all if we give it a chance. It is one of the functions of the housewife to keep chaos at bay – which is also the aim of life altogether, of course. I feel that if I relax too much I will disintegrate. Superficially I am very energetic but deep within myself is an enormous lethargy, which will take over if I don't keep moving.

'I find that life is a great deal easier if I am out of the house for part of the day. Nobody's here, so chaos can't occur. I'm out in the world and I can do all the things I want to do much more quickly, on the way to doing something else and it puts them in their proper place. Now I find I am free during a good many hours of the day and my feet just move much more quickly be-cause I am on my own again.'

The large amount of money earned by James, and the small amounts earned by his wife, all go into a common fund. 'Mary just runs all the money' says James. Or as she puts it, 'James just very honourably banks his salary into a joint account, and I spend it. Sometimes he doesn't even look at the account for months on end. He prefers not to have all the problems of budgeting. I don't really budget, because I'm not very good at that sort of planning. We just sort of go on, and if it seems to be within our income, James is quite happy to leave it to me.

'I don't spend money on myself. James knows that I have had this Protestant background, so that I have these invisible con-trols.' She rolls her eyes, laughing. 'But I do worry about it more than James, because he knows that he is able to produce the money each month, and I know that I can *never* generate this income.'

James likes to think that deep down they are interchangeable, but Mary cannot forget the spectre of the £3000 she feels she would be struggling with if James died or disappeared. He expresses greater confidence in her talents, and is sure that within a brief time she would find some way of using them to earn more. 'Like sleeping with some director?' she enquires with mock bitterness. 'You can't talk in those terms unless you are prepared to sell yourself as a woman in some way.'

Mary isn't quite confident enough to think of her function as cost effective, but says that James has only flung the cost of running their home at her when arguments have become so bitter that it would not have mattered *what* he had said. 'It's rather sweet, he brings home his payslip with a big smile on his face and says, "Oh, it's so many hundreds this month" and he expects me to say, actually say, "Well done, dear" and put it in my pocket and walk off with it. He wants my praise for the fact that he has earned more than usual that month, although it is automatically put into the central fund. But there is no question about who is making the money.'

Mary's job at home is indisputably contributive to what James is doing, although he says that if something terrible happened, if she died or left, he would not be completely lost. 'I would get round it by paying a lot of money, buying my way out of trouble.'

Mary reflects on his requirements and her responsibilities: 'I think the symptom of how James regards me and my role is that he does not have a key to the house. I find that very interesting. He does *not* have a key, and the very rare occasions that he comes home and I'm not here, he can't get in. He can go to my mother up the road and wait. But like as not if she is out, she is with me, shopping. The other day he had to sit across the road with some neighbours for an hour and a half until we came back.'

James does not think that it is worth carrying three keys (they have an elaborate lock and alarm system) for that occasional lock-out. Mary resents the thought that he assumes all is well at home and that she will always be waiting for him. But he says, no, no, no, it's not that, it is just that he associates keys with worry, and there is absolutely no need, so far as he's concerned, for any worry connected with the house. 'No, because you have shelved it on to your wife; if the roof falls in, I'll cope.' She flares, then thinks for a minute. 'Yes, it's true, I would.'

In spite of all this, Mary says that she would only describe herself as a housewife 'under duress'. She had to get a new passport recently and put herself down as a writer, because she couldn't bear to write the word housewife. 'Researcher, I could have put down, or company director, which in Northern Ireland means bookie! Ah well, I suppose we all write from time to time.'

Both appreciate that the balance of life that they have established works within James's home-and-away pattern of existence. Neither can quite imagine what it would be like if he were around seven days a week. He realizes that she does not have much idea what he does all day ('what does the word meeting mean to you?') and she knows that most of what she is doing is invisible to him. They have, they agree, a satisfactorily split day, and enjoy meeting at the end of it.

Once they move out of this ambience, and appear in public as a couple, things are different and more complicated. At a dinner party for instance. 'I feel that James disapproves of me immediately we step outside the walls of this house. There are many times, socially, that I wish he wasn't there, so that I could flaunt myself, be myself completely. But he sits there with disapproval written all over his face. He thinks I come on far too strong, and that I show characteristics that he doesn't admire.'

James admits to these feelings but says that it isn't because he thinks her behaviour is any reflection on him, it's just that he feels she changes her character in public. Or at least alters her outward portrayal of that character, adopting an 'aggressive, almost butch attitude'.

Mary hits back:

'Am I not just expressing things I haven't had an opportunity to express at home? I know that he feels that alcohol and company loosen my tongue unattractively, and that my voice rises by one or two decibels. He thinks I exaggerate to create effect. I think that in a dinner party situation it is acceptable to flirt a little bit, flirt with ideas and images of oneself, and it bounces off other people. I'm not talking in a sexual sense at all.

'There are times, when if your husband wasn't there, you

could put up a much greater show. It would, in a sense, be a falsifying, and it would be an act, but there is no harm in that in certain social circumstances. When James is there watching me, I imagine him ticking off all the things that are not true to my married self. It can sometimes be better to be on your own. There are times when as a woman, quite apart from other social roles that I have, that I would like to let fly, and can't do it because there are certain social images that I am meant to be balancing at the same time . . .'

James denies that he is ever wanting to stop her talking or restrain her character. He just rears back from the aggressive image he thinks she assumes. Mary says that a few years back, before she started working outside the home at all, this might have been true. 'I might have been annoyed and aggressive with people because I was basically unhappy with the role of total housewife I was playing. Now I feel much more at ease, much happier with myself. It used to worry me like anything that I had nothing to say when people asked me what I "did". People are defined by their work and I had no work apart from being a mother and a housewife. I felt utterly spare. Now I do have something to tell, I don't really want to; it seems too aggressive. I'm content to enjoy it.'

Mary knows very well the value of her 'secret' domestic skills but she knows that back in the big heterosexual world, the skills she exercises at home mean nothing at all. 'Domestic life is wonderfully asexual' she says.

'The thing about marriage is that you can let an awful lot of yourself rest; you don't have to every night go through all the challenges again. But when you venture out into the heterosexual world, even for dinner, you are back in a different set of values altogether and other, dormant, parts of yourself are brought out – if you are having any vibrant kind of conversation.'

Mary believes, although she allows emotional chaos to wink at her in such encounters, that marriage, with roles defined more or less to the time-honoured norm, is the most efficient way of living. 'I couldn't bear to share certain areas of my life with other people as part of a communal life, if that was the alternative. Even if I lived alone I would seek some of the same ends. I would have the same fears at the back of my mind. My working towards the maintenance of a style, which is what one is talking about really in domestic organization, setting up a home and so on, comes from things outside marriage. My pursuit of order comes from much further back.'

James, if things collapsed, could live in a hotel, but, as he says, he does sufficient of that already to know that it is a pretty empty life: 'It's very easy, you can pick your breakfast and hang the card over the door and it comes at 7.30 and you have a bath and then eat it and then you go downstairs and the taxi is waiting to take you to the factory. It's an empty life, but it is useful to have it two days a week because all the services are taken care of. To do it permanently, well . . .' The wife and the housewife in particular, humanize his life, while not reducing efficiency.

In the last analysis Mary can find little fault with her situation. Her conflicts, she says, are not between housewifery and extra-domestic work (for work in this context, read freedom, independence) but between motherhood and work. 'Too many people lump the two roles together; I prefer to draw a distinction and I must say that I find the child much more demanding and absorbing. A child, or children, restricts you and determines you emotionally to a much greater extent than being a housewife. I have a substitute housewife at the moment anyway, in that I have a cleaner who also does the ironing, which leaves me with the child care and the cooking, which are areas I am quite happy in. Shopping too, of course, but with a car that is no big thing for a family of three.'

So, the functional part of home life is, the couple agree, a necessary but uninteresting part of life. 'We both' says James, 'need a smug existence on a superficial level. For me, and for Mary to some extent, work is where the action is. Home is a retreat, the quiet place that enables all the rest to happen, helps me to cope with the nastiness, the competition and so on.'

Mary knows well that the 'aggro is elsewhere, and he doesn't want it at home.' At the same time she has her own ground rules. 'I assume that James is fond of me and is not having it off elsewhere. This may be a gross illusion, but I presume that he assumes the same about me. We don't necessarily have to talk to each other a great deal.'

If this illusion was shattered, it would, they agree, be a great threat to the rest of life. 'I would find it very difficult to work' says James. 'I have my own standards all day long at the office; when I come home I relax, and my standards are somehow underneath Mary's.'

His wife, while accepting and enjoying this attitude, sees one danger. 'When I needle him and try to get him to make wild declarations of affection and loyalty and admiration, he just says, Oh, for goodness sake don't go on, because all that kind of sprightliness has gone out of him during the day. And in the morning he is up and shaving and listening to John Timson. I mean, there isn't very much passion left over and so, in a sense, as his wife, I *am* an employee of the company . . .'

Mary talks about herself in an ironic, almost arch way as if afraid to drop the defence of self criticism, even self-mockery for long. But she worried after our conversation that she might have sounded too home-obsessed in answering my questions. She felt I hadn't asked enough about her son, and that she had not sufficiently emphasized the importance of her work. '*They* are the driving forces of my life – my child and my work.'

Stephanie: The Gilded Cage

I wasn't choosing between marriage and a career. I was really thinking of my own peace of mind. I just wasn't happy and I came to realize that there were other possibilities in life . . . I find I can do so much more now. I love upholstery and making curtains. I love creating things for the house.

Stephanie Harrison's husband John is a man for whom the cliche 'dynamic businessman' might have been invented. At thirty-seven he runs his own thriving travel company at a pace that leaves rivals gasping. His wife, on the other hand, has given up a promising career to stay at home. She is thirty, they have been married for five years and don't have children.

She is a housewife although she isn't crazy about the label : 'I don't think of myself as a housewife because it's such an un-flattering term. I prefer to think of myself as a lady who enjoys herself and gets on with life primarily and looks after the house as a secondary thing. "Housewife" to me means somebody who has a terrific routine and who is in the house all the time and possibly has children – who is a homebody in a homespun sort of way. I like to think I'm more sophisticated than that – more middle class and trendy I suppose.

'I gave up work about two and a half years ago. I had a very promising career with lots of travelling, working for a cosmetic company which I suppose is the sort of job lots of girls dream about. I started as a secretary and went into marketing and PR. About six weeks before I was going to leave, I went to a big marketing meeting in France and played quite a big part. When I got back, the managing director called me in and said how pleased they all were with me and I said, "Well, thanks, but I'm going to leave actually." If I had stayed, I don't think I would have become a director because it's such a huge international company, but if I had stayed, it would have been for another year and then I would probably gone and worked for a smaller firm, been a bigger fish in a smaller pond.'

Stephanie said that she found it a great strain combining home with work because of the sort of man she is married to. 'John is quite demanding; he likes the house to look nice; he likes his meals on time and I used to get really, really tired and crash out at about 9.30 on the sofa. Because he's got lots of energy, it used to irritate him. He does so much in one day that he thought I ought to have the same stamina. It made me very, very ratty. I used to spend the lunch hour dashing up to Shepherd's Market for food and then lugging it all home on the tube. Public transport and shopping bags and rainy weather just combined to make life very difficult.

'Then the management of the company changed, and I didn't get on terribly well with the new managing director. He wanted me to give myself entirely to the company, and I just didn't feel at that stage that I could do it. My private life was becoming quite difficult; we were having rows about it and because of that I probably wasn't working as well as I could and the MD kept pushing and pushing me.

'I knew I was under-achieving, so really he had every reason to get at me. I wasn't choosing between marriage and a career – it wasn't as drastic as that. I was really thinking of my own peace of mind. I just wasn't happy and I came to realize that I wasn't a career girl and that there were other possibilities in life.

'It was a sort of test, giving up work, because I knew if I didn't like being at home, I could always get another job. It was an experiment financially too, because John said we would have to see if we could manage without my salary – which was very good. Luckily, his business started to really take off at that point so money ceased to be a problem. I find I can do so much more now. I love my upholstery and making curtains. I love creating things for the house – I get so much pleasure from it and I can do all that now.'

Stephanie does what she calls the bare minimum of housework. 'I make sure the loos and basins are clean and keep everything tidy, but if you ran your finger along the furniture you'd find it very dusty. I like housework when I've done it but I hate thinking about it. I never get up thinking, "I'm going to stay at home all day and do the cleaning." I clean if somebody's coming to stay or coming for dinner. I have no routine at all in my life; every day is totally different. I do the washing when the basket is full and the same with the ironing. I tend to live by deadlines, just like when I was working. I'm always dashing about – always busy. I couldn't tell you what I'm doing but I never stop.'

The big difference for her comes in the evening. 'If I'm here during the day sewing or something, I stop about 5.30 and prepare the dinner. Then we can have a civilized meal together and talk and watch TV, if there is anything worth watching. Before, that was when I had to do all the housework and ironing.

'I'm much more relaxed and much more tolerant of the whole world as a result. I think when you're working, you're more in touch with the outside world – I take an interest in what is going on but I don't take things so seriously any more. I cope with life better if I'm riding along on the surface. I'm not the sort of person who waves banners anyway. It doesn't seem to agree with me – makes me tetchy and jumpy. I'm extremely lucky – I have a relaxing, pleasant life and if I do need a bit of money, then I work for John for a few days manning the phones or doing the books or something.

'If I've been working, John will wash up for me and he'll clean out the fire and help with the garden. If we've got somebody coming and there's a lot to do, then he will buckle to and help but generally, I do most of it. I do all the cooking and washing and ironing. He likes to cook very occasionally, about three times a year; if I'm not feeling very well then he cooks the meal. He always makes the coffee – he's a coffee freak.

'I don't think he understands women very well. He doesn't understand the things that upset us and get us down. He thinks most women are stupid – he really does. He says there are very few women he knows who are "good value" as he puts it. He always says I'm the only person he could be married to because I'm fairly rational. I think the business has a lot to do with it because the girls he employs are a bit scatter-brained and dozy and I think he judges others by them. He's definitely a chauvinist, there's no doubt about it.

'If we go out to parties or dinner, he has no problem talking to the women but he isn't a flirtatious sort of man in any way. He never chats women up; if we broke up it would never be because there was another woman involved. He's not very interested in women romantically.'

Stephanie says John is difficult to live with because he's such a positive person, either all for, or all against, something – never midway. 'He's not very tolerant and I'm very passive now. John has always got a battle on with somebody, whether it's business, or his car, or the garage is no good. He enjoys it though – he loves fighting, it's the way he's always lived his life. He says his philosophy is that he will not allow himself to be ripped off by anybody whether it's going to buy a pint of milk or doing a huge deal with an airline for some tickets. But he's a very fair person and if he thinks anybody's trying to do a dirty on anybody then he gets very upset.'

She reckons he values her most as a companion, as somebody to talk to as an equal. He discusses business with her a lot now, far more than he used to. 'He needs somebody with a fairly good brain so he can test out his ideas.'

John Harrison expects a very well oiled machine at home – everything has to be organized. He doesn't actually interfere with how his wife does things although he's interested in helping to choose the colours of the walls or the curtain material or what to plant in the garden.

'Home' is a large, elegant Victorian house with a walled garden in Richmond, Surrey. 'The house is terribly important to both of us' says Stephanie. 'We spend half our time in the evening gazing round saying, "Isn't it wonderful?" It's a sort of crystallization of your marriage, really, when you find somewhere you love, and you really enjoy living there and you put an enormous amount of energy into getting it the way you want it. We sit in the living room after dinner and look round and exclaim to each other about it and how glad we are that we got this house. We go half and half on ideas. We compromise a lot. If something has to be done and I know how I want to do it and I know he's going to want to do something different, I can see it coming and I have learnt how to manoeuvre him, just like women are supposed to do in order to get their own way in the end.

'John gives me a housekeeping sum every month of £130, which also has to cover hair-dos and tights and things like that. If I need money for curtains or sheets or bigger items like that, then I ask him for however much I need. I normally buy all the birthday presents out of that money as well as all the food and regular household items. I do have some money of my own, a small private income, so I buy all my clothes out of that. I have my own bank account but John pays all the bills. When I was working we used to split everything.

'We don't have a joint account because I think if John got his statement and I had splashed out on a pair of shoes that I didn't necessarily need, he would get annoyed. He's very different from me in that respect. I love clothes and he doesn't care how he looks at all. He's got one suit which he drags out for formal occasions and the rest of the time he wears a selection of about three pairs of baggy cords.

'We don't argue about money. He thinks I'm a bit extravagant but it never comes to anything. To begin with I did mind being given housekeeping but I've got used to it now. I got a rise in January, the first in two and a half years and I was dreading asking for it but he was absolutely fine about it.

'I suppose I must be influenced by advertising when I'm shopping. But I very rarely change brands of things, though. I use Persil in the washing machine because my mother always used it I think. I tried one of those biological powders but I didn't like it much and then I read that it damages your lungs if you breathe it in so I don't use it now. I'm perfectly aware of the money that is spent on trying to influence people like me but because I've been involved in that business I'm fairly cynical about it. That was one side of my job I really did not like – I hated the people I came across in the business. We get lots of door drops here. I got a load of coupons for Persil the other day but I just throw them away.

'John and I are terrific friends. I can't think of anybody I'd rather have dinner with than John. We talk a lot about all sorts of things. He's a very interesting person – good to be around, very stimulating. He's very interested in the world which is good for me because otherwise I would shut myself off a bit. He's very good at getting on with people so I never have to worry about how he's going to behave at dinner parties. He's given me a lot of confidence since we've been married; I've changed a lot. I think I've become more interesting because he's drawn me out.

'He's a terribly organized person. He has to have his jerseys on one shelf and his shirts on another and so on. He gets very concerned if the washing basket gets full and he might run out of clean underwear. He likes everything to be just so.' After making everything 'just so' Stephanie pursues her other interests.

'Upholstery is my main hobby at the moment, and through that I've become very interested in antiques. I don't know a lot about it but I buy lots of books and then test myself out by looking in antique shop windows and identifying things. I go to upholstery classes every week for three hours. That's also made me interested in soft furnishings. I'm fascinated by fabrics.

'I'm also very keen on cooking. Food plays a major part in my life. I read cookery books for pleasure. I enjoy entertaining and I'd like to give more dinners. I like to have everything just right and make really nice things. I love riding, too, but I don't get much chance to do that any more. I used to work in a stable and we think that perhaps one day we'll move to the country and have horses. I play tennis in the summer and ski in the winter. Gardening is a great obsession, although ours isn't done properly yet. I love talking about plants and looking up things I want to plant.

'I think John was a bit worried about me giving up my career to become a housewife. I think he was quite proud of the sort of job I had. When he first met me he thought I was some really big-wig – the image was soon shattered, I can tell you. I think he liked me having such a good job. The minute I gave up my job I had the offer of a very part-time one with a travel agency, and he really pushed me to take it. I think he thought I was going to sit at home and not do anything. He knew I was unhappy with work so he said, make a complete change and see if it makes you better. If it doesn't we'll think again. He was very good about all that because I had been boring him for months with tales of woe about work. He said, for God's sake leave. Do something about it.

'I hate people asking me what I 'do' at parties. I say I'm a housewife. Then I say that I sometimes work for my husband. I don't want them to think I'm a slut who sits around in her dressing-gown all day. I do feel odd about it, but the whole thing is so ridiculous. I could just as well say I'm a gardener since I spend so much time doing the garden.

'Nobody seems to think it odd that I stay at home but don't have children. People tend to ask me straight if we are trying to start a family and when I say, yes, that seems to make it alright. I suppose the people we mix with are from our age group and class, and they don't seem to question how we live. The only people who have expressed surprise are members of my family – aunts, and uncles. They talk about it to my mother. They think it's a bit funny that we don't have children but not that I don't work. None of them ever did; when they got married, they gave up work. I'm sure they think I'm infertile or have some kind of problem.

'Other people are quite accepting of the way we live, partly I think because we go away a lot to see to John's business. That was another big reason for giving up work – I wanted to be able to travel with him. I have lunch occasionally with the people I used to work with and I think they think, "Bloody cheek, she's off enjoying herself." I'm convinced it's just envy, however. I think an awful lot of people would like to be in my position. I don't encounter direct resentment from people, but I do find myself constantly apologizing for not working because I realize how lucky I am and that other people have a terribly hard life. I don't say much about what I do or don't do all day. I don't want to upset people, particularly friends. I'd hate to lose friends by appearing to be complacent.

'But I do like my role as it is. I don't want to spoil it by having children. I mean, I'd like to have them, I'd like the whole selfish thing of growing old with a family growing up around me and grandchildren etc. But at the moment I can think of nothing more guaranteed to spoil my life than a kid. I mean, it wouldn't spoil my life exactly but it would certainly alter it.

'I'm very conscious of time; I love to feel that my time is my own. I like being on my own. Having worked to deadlines all my working life, I appreciate the freedom I have now all the more. It is very satisfying to plan a day, in the same way as you would if you had to go to several meetings and a lunch, and to know at the end of it that you have achieved all the tasks you set out to do. It's just the same as working really. I make a mental list of all the things I want to get done and do them. I've got my own car now, John bought it for my birthday, which has made a big difference to my life. I'm completely independent. I don't have to ask John if I can "borrow the car"; not that he didn't want me to have it before but I know it irritated him because I had to change the seat and mirror and so on.

'I don't like to bother John. I mean, he has a very busy, difficult life and I try to – not keep out of the way exactly – but not upset him because he's very easily upset. I like to think that I create a serene, comfortable atmosphere for him to relax in when he comes home. I like to make sure everything looks nice when he comes home.

'I don't worry any more about what I look like. I go around in really mucky jeans for days on end and then dress up for a day or two. I used to have loads of clothes and make up very carefully. I don't wash my hair as often now and I'm sure people can't believe their eyes if they come to the door when I'm doing my upholstery, wearing filthy rolled up jeans and old wellingtons. I feel much more relaxed – I'm not competing in a competitive world any more. I know a lot of women lose confidence when they give up work to stay at home, usually with children, but it's been exactly the reverse for me.

'I don't miss the competitive world of business at all. I get all my satisfaction from doing things to the house – it has replaced the job in a way I suppose. When somebody comes in and admires the curtains I've made for the sitting room, it's just like being told I've done a good report. I don't feel the job done is any less rewarding because I don't get paid a wage for doing it – money doesn't come into it. That's because of John really. He's a bit awe-inspiring – quite frightening when he starts thumping the table about something but he's marvellous to me – spoils me rotten.

'I don't give any active support to the feminist movement. It's one of those selfish things really. It's never bothered me. I've always managed to get on with men and women and within reason, I've always got what I wanted. If I haven't got what I wanted it hasn't been because a man has stopped me, but because of my own mistakes. I've never really come up against discrimination and I've never felt underprivileged – I've never had to fight those sort of battles. I'm a bit complacent about it really; I subscribe to the view that if you want something, you can get it. I know that there are a lot of women stuck at home doing homeworker type jobs which are very badly paid but it hasn't affected my life; I don't think about it too much. If anything, talk about women's lib makes my life more difficult. If I come home complaining about carrying heavy shopping bags, John just throws it back at me. If I did give active support to women's liberation, it would be to support middle aged wives and mothers whose children had left home – the sort of women who get about £10 a week housekeeping and their husbands go out every night and spend the rest in the pub. Those are the sort of women who need women's lib.

'My great hope for the future is that our marriage continues to be as good as it is now – and gets better. We have both mellowed in the last couple of years and get on terribly well now.'

Margaret: Light in the Corner Shop Window

> I had always wanted to do something. You see I'm not one of
> those housewives that liked housework and that kind of thing.
> It just drives me mad stopping in all day . . .

Margaret Elliot lives in Sunderland, one of the bleakest towns of
the bleak North East, where the men are in and out of work with
the tide of industrial fortune. The people have learned to expect,
if not to accept, this kind of seesaw; the wit and spirit of the
region is as famous as its industrial depression.

Margaret is twenty-eight, the wife of a bricklayer. In
December 1976, with a group of friends and sisters-in-law, she
founded a small grocery co-operative called Little Women.

Margaret explains: 'We talked about the idea for maybe two
years before we opened. It took us that long to raise the money.
But when we opened it was in a blaze of publicity. We didn't
have a clue what to do, you know. None of us had worked in a
shop before, so it was a bit mind boggling . . . all the telly
cameras here and everything. After a few weeks we got on our
feet.

'I had always wanted to do something. You see, I am not one
of those housewives that like housework and that type of thing.
It just drives me mad stopping in all day . . . so I just thought of
it one night in bed, the idea of the shop and the bench for old
people to sit on, and the room for the kids upstairs. That was it,
it just came to me one night when I was thinking, now, what
sort of shop? And food was the natural thing because we all
need to buy food ourselves, and that would be some takings. It
doesn't matter how flat broke you are, you've got to eat.

'I thought of my friends, the ones that I thought would like the idea, be committed and so on. I approached my sister-in-law Barbara and my friends and they were interested, because with all the kids being small there was no way of going to work unless we paid the money out to baby minders, and we didn't fancy that. At least here the bairns can be with us.' (When the shop started most of the kids were about two years old, but some, like Margaret's eldest daughter, were already at school.)

The co-operative notion hit Margaret Elliot after her husband Peter started working at Sunlandia, a big building co-operative in Sunderland. 'We had never really heard of co-operatives or common ownership before that. When he got into it, we both thought that was how things ought to be done.'

So 'the girls' started meeting, and Margaret joined ICOM, the Industrial Common Ownership Movement. 'We are not political at all. There's a couple of labour voters and a couple of liberals and a couple of conservatives mixed in there as well. If you asked the lasses, they'd say "I vote Labour". But they wouldn't say "I'm a socialist". We tend to keep away from that side of things. If people thought we were socialists and they were conservatives they would say, "Well, I'm not going to shop there." '

They used to meet once a month at the pub; they now meet monthly in each other's homes. Margaret started writing away to trusts, visiting bank managers and building societies. 'I got refused most of the time. We needed £8,500 to get it off the ground and we didn't have any money of our own to put in. We had to borrow it all. The first money came from ICOM.

'One of the girls went to London and put our ideas forward. They agreed to lend us £500 as a starter, then £500 when we opened. We got another £1000 which came from interested parties who lent through ICOM. Then we met this man, John Morton, from Commonwork Trust. They've got a big farm and eventually they want to have shops of their own. They agreed to lend us £3000 (lucky, because after that loan the Trust changed its policy, and it no longer helps to launch new ventures).

'We went to a bank manager at the National Westminster Bank, and he was very interested. All the others had said, "We realize that in the future this is going to be commonplace, but it's a bit too risky at the moment because nobody has done any-

G

thing like it before." But the Nat West man was different and John Morton went to see him which was a lot of trouble for him, all the way from London. He agreed to loan us £2,500. But we had to get our husbands to sign as guarantors, because we weren't working. It's common policy I suppose. All the husbands signed and that was it.

'We found the premises. It was an old butcher's shop. There wasn't a shelf or anything in it; all the floors needed to be renewed. It was dropping to bits really, so we all got in on that. We had a month to get it ship-shape so that we could open in time to catch the Christmas trade. The husbands helped us because we can't lay floors very well and they put up shelves. They all dug in. The night before we opened my husband was just putting the sign up.'

It was Margaret's husband who thought up the name. 'Oooh, he gets his neb in doesn't he?' said his wife, giggling. 'We were thinking of "The Company We Keep", and things like that. He says "how about Little Women, because it'll make people think – because you're not little, and it catches the imagination." He said "How about that then?" and I said "ooh" and that's how it came about.

'We had to get registered. We did it under the Friendly Societies Act which is cheap. If we had registered as a limited company, it would have meant a lot of legal formalities.'

In fact they did afterwards become a limited company. 'We had to be, with us being women, with us not having any money anyway. If we'd gone down the dilly we couldn't have found the money to pay everyone back. But we haven't and we don't intend to!

'When we opened in that blaze of publicity we thought the customers would be queuing outside the door, but it takes a long time for people to change their shopping habits. We used to just sit and wait. They used to come in and say, "I thought you were going to be cheap". People got the idea that we were trying to sell things without making any profit at all. We do try to keep things low, but we can't compete with supermarkets. Over the months we gradually picked up a good bunch of regular shoppers. We've built up a good reputation for cooked meats and that. There was a Liptons shop a few doors down and their prices were very low but they had to close down because it wasn't viable for them and they kept getting broken into. That meant our takings shot up. We've got a steady turnover now. It took us a long time to get a system worked out – how to handle the mark up, what to do with special offers and how to work out the jobs. But we've got a good one going now.'

They buy from a warehouse, and a cash and carry. Margaret passed her driving test so the cash and carry run is her job. 'Things like pies and bread are delivered every morning. In the shop there is a name over every section of the shelving. Each girl is responsible for a section of the shelving, to keep it stocked, to price it correctly and order new stuff. Every three months we change jobs, so I'm doing the back yard at the moment and Brenda is scrubbing the floor and so on with keeping the stockroom and the rooms upstairs.

'I started the books off, and then I showed Kath how to do them. Now we've all had a turn. So everybody knows about every aspect of the business, which was my dream because I thought, it's no good if somebody is off sick and leaves everybody up in the air. As it is nobody's indispensable. Everybody knows all the jobs.'

Margaret describes the shop simply as a small grocers. 'We like the personal touch, we like to talk to our customers. We know most of them by their first names and they know us. We may not be the cheapest, but people don't feel obliged to rush in and out again. They can stay and have a good laugh with us. You get a lot of pensioners around here and they can just get what they need for their tea – you know, a couple of sausages or a quarter of butter. It's amazing how many do that. In the supermarket things are mostly prepacked in larger amounts. They used to feel awful asking for a couple of eggs and a slice of bacon, but they know now that we don't mind. We get a lot of housewives who go into town to do their main shopping and pop in here for their bread and bacon and cooked meats because they like that. Our big customers are the ones who can't be bothered going to town so they come in and place a big order every week.

'We work a three-week rota, and each of us works, say twenty to twenty-five hours a week. There's three girls in at any one time – when the kids are here there's one up looking after them and two in the shop. It changes every hour, because an hour is about just enough when you've got six kids charging about. They all come here for their dinners and then again after school – at least we go and fetch them. That's all quite recent, most of them have just started school. We don't know what to do with ourselves, only having them for a couple of hours.'

Whatever else Margaret and her friends get out of the enterprise, it isn't riches. They take 50 pence an hour each as wages, for a twenty-one hour week and use it to supplement their housekeeping money. 'We have come to rely on it though, says Margaret. We need that extra few pounds.

'We open at nine every morning. If the three girls on duty have to take the kids to school, then it's 9.30 but we can't help that – we've got to take the bairns to school. At dinner time one person just goes and gets them all, but in the morning we like to see our kids into school ourselves and give them a kiss and that.'

Fitting home life around the shop has not been difficult in the way that ordinary jobs would have been. The women's husbands have been basically in favour and offered support – although they have been twinges of jealous resentment at their wives' absorption in something independent. It has been an upheaval but only one woman has dropped out because of commitments at home.

'I do tend to be full of the shop all the time. Your conversation tends to revolve around it. I get in about ten to six on my work nights – at the most three a week. He doesn't have to worry about the bairns because they are with us. It works out quite well that way.

'But we do tend to live around the shop. Most of the husbands are very good about it. They get a bit sick of it at times, I think. The shop is a real part of our lives now, you know, and I think they get a bit jealous.' There is really only one part of the job the women take home with them. 'Whoever does the books has to take them home – which takes up a canny bit of your time. But the rest of it is done at the shop. The work doesn't really encroach on the husband's time. But they feel sometimes as if we're pushing them out, and we've got to work hard at overcoming that.'

All of the partners felt strongly that they had to 'get out of the house' but the shop has not in any way cut down their domestic commitments. 'My husband doesn't help at home because he works very hard, so I don't really expect him to. On a Sunday, if he's off, he'll dry the dishes for us. But I don't expect him to have my tea ready if he's home before me, because he's absolutely shattered. Mind, if he wasn't working, I would. There's quite a few of us had our husbands on the dole with the situation the way it is here. There's often one or two of them on the dole and then they have the tea ready. But they don't have the house sparkling! They're not like that, but they never have been, so . . . But we all find the housework less of a bind now; we don't do as much cleaning and the house is just as clean. That's because we're not in it as much.

'Things get a bit hectic during the six weeks holiday period in the summer. You have to work extra hours because there may be two people off. Also you've got the kids here all the time. We take them out to the beach and the park. It is the hardest time of the year. When they go back to school in September everybody breathes a sigh of relief.

'In the beginning, we had a few personality clashes but you learn to put up with it and accept people for what they are. You've got to otherwise it wouldn't work. Working the whole system out was trial and error right along the line. For instance, we used to run a special offer, run out and we'd still have the bill stuck on the window. It took us a long time to evolve the jobs, and we feel now, that we've got it right.'

She is, however pleased, not carried away by their first success. 'We'll pay off our debts before planning too much for the future. In the beginning the dream was to open other common ownerships. Barbara always wanted to be a hairdresser but she doesn't want to now. We thought we'd pay for her to get trained and she could open a common ownership hairdressers. Then we thought we could have a launderette and a boutique, and things like that. In reality, it doesn't work out like that. We do want to move onto other things but it's going to take a few years.'

There was a time when Margaret Elliot felt she had bitten off more than she could chew. 'In the beginning, I felt the onus was on me to make it work. I felt I had to be in on everything and I nearly worked myself to a frazzle. I had to delegate in the end because if I hadn't I would have been dead now, I think. It's very difficult delegating when it's your thing. Once I realized what I was doing wrong and it didn't take long really, it was okay. People could do the jobs just as well as me. Now I know that none of the decisions are mine entirely. I've always got others to talk it over with.'

The meetings between the members of the co-operative, held in turn at their respective homes, are vital: 'We have truth sessions. If somebody isn't doing the job right, then we tell them – but they've not to take it badly. We can't afford to let somebody lag behind while we do all their work for them. Often you find that there are problems at home or the person may be run down, and we can try to help.'

The women give their new found co-operative strength back to the community as well: they hold an annual general meeting every year and give a party afterwards for all their customers. 'We hire a room, and a disco, and the girls make hundreds of sandwiches and sausage rolls and we all have a great time.'

Anna: The Difficult Tandem

> The balance with your husband has to be constantly renegotiated. It's not a balance you just set out at the beginning, because the age of the child – all sorts of things – alter it. You can't insist on exact sharing at any one time.

Anna Fuller was an active member of the early women's movement in Britain, and has tried very hard to practise what she has preached. With her husband Peter, she has put the feminist ideals of equal sharing and equal opportunity to the test in her own marriage.

Anna is now in her mid-thirties, and well established as an anthropologist, working in a highly difficult but prestigious field, studying domestic life in China. Her husband is also an academic, teaching engineering at a University. They now have two children, Daniel and Louise, who were aged five years and nine months respectively at the time of this interview.

London is the family base, where the Fullers own two floors of a large Edwardian house in Highgate, but their careers require travel. Anna has been to China several times, and her present job is really in Geneva; she is doing a study for the United Nations of food production at domestic level in China. The family has spent the past year in the United States where Peter was on a sabbatical at Princetown. Anna talked to me, while they were home on a working visit, about the sharing pattern they have evolved and continued through the birth and rearing of the children.

'We were married for nine years before we had Daniel. It is very easy to share when you don't have children, there is not the day to day negotiation. If the beds don't get made one day, it doesn't matter. But when there is a child involved, if he is not delivered somewhere or fed then it *does* matter. That's when the crunch of sharing really comes.'

The crunch for Anna and Peter came at a particularly testing moment for her. 'Conceiving Daniel was accidental. Probably the time was right, but it was a great surprise. I didn't even consider an abortion, because I reckoned we would have got round to it in the next two years anyway and what's two years? And I did a very strange thing – I didn't really find out that I was pregnant until it was almost too late. Now I just maintain that it was the best accident we ever made.'

It was the precise state of her career that made the timing of the baby so tough for Anna. 'Although I had a career, I had really just found myself in terms of what I wanted to do. With my professional interest in China and my great interest in feminism, I was able to write a book about feminism in China. For a long time you work at a book and there comes a time when in your head you have to think of nothing else, otherwise it never gets finished. There is that hump, and the book has to take you over. That was the hump, just when Daniel was born.'

An added complication was the job that came up around the same moment, to do research for a PhD. 'I had come to a particular point when I had been working from home, working on the book, and it wasn't at the time really very fashionable to work on women (I was looking at domestic life, when everyone else was looking at the rostrum to see who would replace Mao; now of course it is so trendy). So the job that I won made all the difference, it put me clear into the professional academic world. I was the same person, it was the same work, but I had a structure, I had a title. Now, Daniel was born in August and the job started in October, and I had to keep the two going. Nobody at the academic institution which had taken me on knew he was coming. If they had, it has been confirmed since, I would not have got the job. I was the first woman to get a job there, and a married woman at that, and I felt a very great responsibility, because if I messed that up, that wasn't going to be very good for those coming behind me. My world is a man's world. That was reinforced all the time by people holding me up as a model, so that I couldn't let go.

'You've got to remember I had my child rather a long time ago compared to the feminists who have had them in the past two or three years. Having children then, in the women's movement, was really quite frowned upon. I was embarrassed. The only way it was kind of accepted was because it was an accident. Now, of course, it has turned right around. My peers are now trying to have children and make it work. You see, they are at that crunchy age – over thirty, and getting to a stage where they do think time is running out. But they are always looking for quite the right year. They are trying to plan it for a year when they can maximize the chances to do both. They would perhaps try not to do it in the first year of a new job, like I did, for instance.

'So, when we knew that Daniel was coming and I was going for this job we realized that we did have to work out some kind of timetable. We spent *hours* working out timetables, which of course never materialized, because we didn't know what the demands were going to be – you never do before any new baby arrives. We were very fortunate with our jobs. I don't think I could have done it with a job where I had to clock in at nine in the morning. The kind of jobs we have had as academics are very privileged.'

Anna and Peter had not previously laid plans about what they would do when they had a child: 'One of the reasons why we put off having children is that we didn't think we could manage it; we didn't know anybody who did manage it, without, say, having a live-in au pair, and we never really considered that as an option. I didn't want to exploit another woman by having her living in the house to look after my child.

'People who know me now think I have had everything very easy. They think I am combining everything – husband, job, family. But it was a real struggle and a gamble. Who knew that it was going to turn out like this? I suffer a bit from people saying well, you *are* lucky.

'We were keen to work out a way in which I could have a child and enjoy it and at the same time keep my own interests. I have a very strong personality, and I suppose I was a little nervous of trying to live too much of a child's life. So I thought if I could keep something for myself, as I always had done before in the marriage, it would be all right.

'I suppose I was afraid, really, of losing my place in the world, and becoming too wrapped up in my children, very wrapped up in my children's education and all that, which I really don't like to see in other people, and I just know that I am no different from most people. I might easily have become obsessed with their educational standards. I mean, I care if they are fitting in at school, but I don't care if they are reading *this* book or *that* book at any particular point. An early starter, is an early starter, is an early starter. So what?

'I decided consciously *not* to breastfeed Daniel, because I felt that I couldn't do everything perfectly. There was no way I could do a job perfectly, run a home perfectly, and bring up a child perfectly, with no other help except Peter, and so that is the kind of decision I did make. I am not sure that it was the right decision in retrospect, but you can see the kind of thinking: if I was adding this new dimension to my life there was no way that I could maintain the standards right across the board. Also we felt strongly that we should share right from the beginning, because that is when the patterns are created. Peter was equally keen to feed this baby as I was; we both went into it trying to do as much as possible. If I had been breastfeeding it would automatically weight it in a different manner. With the second child I did breastfeed, because not doing so the first time backfired on me a bit, and because when there were two children we both had our hands full. With the first child you are both very keen to do things; when there is one each, you don't have time to think, "what shall I do now?"

'The way I think it backfired with me was that Peter was *so* good with Daniel and we shared it to *such* an extent, that I had a bit of depression about three months later and instead of being indispensable, like most new mothers are supposed to feel, I felt completely dispensable in my head. I didn't feel necessary, and felt that if something happened to me, Peter and Daniel could have got on quite well without me.'

Anna laughed a lot about this memory but it was clearly a very painful one. 'I talked to Peter about it, but it had quite severe repercussions because I had a biopsy for breast cancer

192

three months after that and it all seemed ... well it was just a very tough time. I suddenly wondered if we had created this new pattern and that there was a reason for it all, and the reason was that I wasn't going to be around for very long. I thought I was going to die. Part of it was that we had tried to establish this new pattern and I didn't have a lot of company in doing it, there weren't many others, so it did feel pretty lonesome.

'I used to have a theory that every woman should work; this was a long time ago – a half-baked Engelian theory about entering social production you know, all that. It didn't take me very long to realize that if you had the choice of staying at home and looking after your child, or working behind a Sainsbury's till, you would be daft to do the latter unless you really *have* to.'

Anna admitted that, of course, it all rather depended on what the situation at home was like, and that it was easy to forget and transpose your own situation at home with that of the woman who might find going out to work behind a till a way of escaping total isolation. 'All the same, I have come to the conclusion that you've got to be pretty keen on your work to keep it going after you have children, to want to pay the price, to keep wanting to – even after the first flush of the first nine months, to actually maintain it year in and year out. You've really got to be pretty keen.

'The balance with your husband has to be constantly renegotiated. It's not a balance you just set out at the beginning, because the age of the child – all sorts of things – alter it. Periodically timetables change, demands change. You can't insist on exact sharing at any one time. Maybe someone has a deadline to meet, and that is one priority. If your relationship is strong and you are communicating enough, you just have to have faith and say, OK, this is a bad week for Peter. Next week will be my turn. There is no good in saying it *shall* be like this, and then getting all upset when it doesn't turn out that way. Sometimes one has to think in terms of *years*. My experience of marriage has been nothing but supportive and that has given me a modicum of independence. I think I have been able to do things that some of my unmarried friends have not been able to do. Because, for example, I was able to go back to university and it didn't matter if I had a grant or not. I have no compunction about living on

Peter's salary for a year because in other ways I have contributed more. I don't have hangups about that.

'I know I made a big decision this year that I would do more, and that Peter would do less in the home, because I felt that he had done a great deal in the last three or four years, to the cost of one or two of his projects which had not quite got over the hump. This seemed a way of saying "thank you" for all the support he had given me. I mean, I wrote my PhD thesis and finished a book, and had a lot of priorities. And every time I had to go abroad, because I won't go without the children, we all had to go. So I expect him to jump up and lose his work vacation and come to Hong Kong because I am going to China, or come to Geneva because I've got to go there. It's all very nice and we have lovely times, but I am making a demand. Therefore, when he decided he wanted to go to America I said I would come and try to do a lot more domestically.

'I dislike intensely the pattern where people talk about decision-making as a couple and the man says, "oh yes I make all the big decisions about who's going to invade who, and I leave all the small ones about which school to my wife". I just want to sock him one. It is not just a question of division of labour, but of both doing it. It is quite a different thing for him to sit there and read the paper and decide what's going to happen in the world next.'

So, Peter and Anna share domestic labour and child care, rather than dividing it, and the timetable is by no means rigid. Anna tried to recreate how they had set about operating their 'pattern' to begin with : 'With Daniel, Peter did all the nights for the first two weeks, to give me time to get back on my feet, because I was starting this job. Then there was one day a week each when one of us was totally responsible for the baby at home. Other days we must just have worked it out. In the morning when we were all trying to get out of the house, it was just all go, so it was both of us doing nothing else but just getting out of the house with Daniel. We would usually take turns to go over to the crèche at lunchtime to feed him. Then you came home at six and everybody was tired and there was Daniel to feed and get to a bath and bed. It was not a question of one of us sitting at a desk, and the other being down there with Daniel, it was a question of both of us working together when necessary. I used to look back on those days when we came home and sat down and had a cup of coffee and then had a leisurely meal. We both tried to enjoy him in the evenings, and at weekends, because if the child had been at the crèche all day, we felt strongly that he needed us and we wanted to be with him. That is something you don't anticipate. I remember hoping that, because I kept my work going, the maternal ties wouldn't be so strong. I have been quite amazed at how strong they are. When people say you should breastfeed your baby to bond the two of you, I just laugh. I couldn't stand any *more* bonding. I spent quite a long time trying to fight it all, until I think I've just given up fighting it really. At the weekend, when we avoid academic work (except sometimes on Saturday night if we are not going out), we try to do things all together, and, as much as possible, play, but I can't give you a clear timetable. On weekdays, as a common courtesy, we both try to be home at six, because everybody's tired and hungry, and that's the really low point when you are on your own. Sometimes I feel a bit resentful, because if I have to be out I always try to leave a meal waiting, so that Peter doesn't have to do that as well as the children. But I have to say, that when *he* goes out *I* don't find a meal waiting!

'I am in no way holding up what we do as a fifty-fifty deal, but I think we share more than most couples, especially the child care. I do think though that I plan more ahead, and I do a lot more in my head. I think that Peter slightly feels that is unnecessary; he's just as capable of going down to the shops at five o'clock and bringing something home. I maintain that is probably more expensive, and less nutritious. But then I want to plan, I want to maintain that control. And I can't have it all ways – I can't have the control (I mean, Peter is not the menial labourer) and the sharing. I am not for a moment claiming that we have an absolutely worked-out programme. There are things that each of us does on the fringes of a common area. He does an awful lot around the house. He's very good at mechanical things. When do I ever go out and get under the car? When do I ever go out and mow the lawn? I don't. So if I start to feel slightly resentful I just have to keep reminding myself of all the things I simply don't do.'

195

Was Peter ever 'slightly resentful'? 'I think he has a fantasy that he will come home and find meals cooked. I think he feels that his colleagues have a tremendous advantage, being serviced, and it *must* help having someone behind you who is servicing you. But it is all a matter for negotiation. I am a little confused about it at the moment because we have been travelling and are not in a routine. You are not always confident, once you get out of the routine, that you will be able to re-establish it.'

Anna said that the thing that had allowed sharing to work for them, insofar as it has worked, was the university crèche. 'We used it for Daniel from three months, two or three days a week. (Our jobs allowed us to have one full day at home each with the child, or children.) I am, intellectually, absolutely for crèches. Emotionally I find it quite difficult to put a child into it five days, nine to five. Before I was married, and before I had children, I was all for twenty-four hour nurseries; I am not sure now what the answer is. If you find a third person who can help care for the children that you are very happy with, perhaps. I was a little nervous about finding the one person, about the gamble involved in choosing one.

'The crèche is hard work. You take the food, you take the child into town. The times I have carried an eighteen-month baby home in the tube, at five o'clock, standing, thinking if I don't get home I will burst into tears. On the other hand to begin with I liked the idea of Peter, Daniel and I all going to the University together in the morning.'

And Daniel? She laughed: 'Oh, he never knew anything else. Also it was very important for him to be with other children. I thought at the time that he might be an only child. And I *believe* in the crèche. I believe in the socialized solution, not just a nanny and an au pair. For my own peace of mind too, it was important that I knew where that child was. If you have someone in your house to look after your child you can't say "stay home", you can't expect someone to sit isolated in someone else's home. But I didn't particularly want someone driving around with my child, or meeting their friends in Muswell Hill. I was quite keen to know that he was at the crèche. There was a certain security in that. I felt there were controls too ... other mothers coming and going. You are pretty quick, aren't you, to pick up reverberations? Also, all of us, by ourselves, get sick of a child. But in any group situation there are other children they can go off with, or there is another mother, or person, you can turn to and say, "take him". But if you have someone alone with the child what sort of outlooks have they got that can be very happy ones?'

Anna kept returning to the fact that all this was made possible by the nature of her work. If she had had a nine to five job, or one of them had, it would have meant more outside help was needed. But the crèche solution is much criticized: 'You get as much flack from women as from men on the subject of crèches. I found it quite hard when Daniel went; even friends who had children, and opted for the private solution, were terribly scornful of me going to the crèche. They really prided themselves on the fact that at least their child didn't have to go to the crèche. I did find that interesting, and a bit hurting at times, because that wasn't exactly the most supportive thing to say to someone who's got a very small baby. And I suppose that's why I was secretly rather pleased that Daniel only had to go three days a week because I still felt that he had four days at home. But you know women look down on crèches, even women in the women's movement who like them in theory. I have a friend who went and worked in a Council crèche and that finished her. No longer could she chant "twenty-four hour nurseries". She really was a bit appalled at what she saw. Even this time, with Louise, a friend at the Tavistock said to me, don't let Louise go to the crèche, get someone in, it's much better for her to have a one-to-one relationship.

'Likewise, I made the decision about not breastfeeding with a certain amount of equanimity. But as soon as I had made it, you couldn't pick up a Sunday newspaper without being told that you were depriving your child for life by not breastfeeding it. So I did suffer a lot of guilt feeling about that. Going against the prevailing ideology is always hard, it's undermining.'

Prevailing ideology now says that mothers should be with their children. If a mother is with her child then all will be well. But the battering figures alone show that this ain't necessarily so. I put it to Anna that everything, surely, in dealing with and rearing children is a compromise, a balancing act.

197

'Yes, it is indeed a balancing act, and I am constantly castigating myself because I have got a bit off balance, for caring too much about my work, and therefore not spending enough time with my children. Or I am perhaps giving them too much attention, and not giving enough to the work. I think that Peter and I both feel that we have got to narrow our lives somewhat for this period. We used to do a lot of things together, like going to political meetings and going to the movies. We used to go to the opera a tremendous amount. But if you bring a child home from the crèche at six, there is no way you are going to turn round and dash out again at half past seven to the opera. It doesn't worry us particularly, but we do feel that we have become less extrovert, less interesting people. But I don't actually mean narrowed because there is a whole new area now which is child orientated. And, being in our thirties, we have no regrets at the change. We have travelled and done all sorts of things. We had a super ten years together, absolutely marvellous. And we still travel, which doesn't make life easy, but is very interesting.

'I am not discontented in any way, I am just, personally, beginning to realize that perhaps *I* have become too narrow. There is another reason for that. I have become very fearful and anxious about life and death, and I think that is the result partly of having children. It started with seeing Daniel and Peter in control and that biopsy (which turned out to be benign). I think I have got over it all right, but it really had preyed on my mind, that lump.

'It was also partly post natal depression, which immediately came when I finished the book. It was make or break just when Daniel was born. Well I slogged at it and I finished it. Then I felt that *I* was finished. I was obviously drained of everything, child, book, the lot. And really I had been a very happy-go-lucky getting-high-on-lemonade type girl before that. Then suddenly there was this terrific anxiety about death, and I really haven't managed to cope with that. I really was very upset at myself. Funnily enough I think it is fairly common among young mothers, because when I admit it to anyone they seem to have it too. A friend who is a professional anthropologist with children and seems fine said, "Oh, I was down at the BUPA place to have tests every month for stomach cancer". She didn't have stomach cancer after all, but she was convinced that she did. She was doing research too. I have actually decided that one of the changes I may have to make is to take a teaching job which would be less isolating than research. Research has been terrific because it has enabled me to combine children and work and keep going – I had flexibility, and children in good health, which makes a big difference. We have had one week in the whole of these years in which Daniel had mumps, and because I didn't have to be anywhere at a specific time I could cushion that, and Peter could relieve me. When the school was on strike I simply started my day at four. So there have been real spin-offs. But the trade-off is between flexibility and isolation, and I think I have got to get out, and get a job where I won't be so isolated or anxious and introverted.'

When it came to the second child the sharing patterns were already well established, and Anna thinks that she relaxed a lot more because in those four years between she had actually established herself: 'I didn't feel any more that I was just at that crucial point and that if I let go that would be it. I am much more relaxed about my work and much more aware what a short period babyhood is and that it is only something that is going to happen once or twice in a lifetime and must be treasured. Peter and I still share but I do a bit more. That is partly choice because I realize that I am the one who is deprived. I think our whole way of thinking is slightly turned, because before, with Daniel, we used to think that the time had been slightly wasted via a vis work. Now we feel quite sorry for people who haven't spent more time with their children. They have deprived themselves of something.

'I am actually much more efficient in terms of my academic work now. When I go and sit at my desk, I can't puddle. I have produced far more since I had a child than before. It is just the discipline of knowing that you haven't got all day and all night. Those days when you are a student and the whole day stretched ahead . . .'

Anna is a little disappointed that so many feminists have gone right back into 'the earth mother image' when she had tried to create a different kind of thing. 'I don't think that people are

H

any longer trying to work out new ways of having children and jobs, or even sharing with blokes.'

One woman she knows who had her children a long time ago, before the women's movement, found she couldn't really talk about her children and their problems at women's groups and meetings. Now she feels quite resentful when she sees feminists having babies and indulging themselves somewhat. She feels slightly cheated, and Anna sympathizes.

'I know that I felt, in a much more minor way that I was really going to indulge myself with Louise, because with Daniel I had to slightly push him on the side, because I was getting on with the main business of work.'

Work outside the home seemed like salvation to the early feminists, but there has been a shift. Anna recalled Juliet Mitchell giving a first hint of it in a television programme some years back. She said, 'It's time that society put reproduction in the first place, not production.' In other words let's give more time to our children and looking after them and not so much to the productive work side.

'Work,' says Anna firmly, 'can only take you so far. You might give your work priority for a while and then if you look back on it, take a space, and look back on it you think well, so what? I mean you can write a book and it can be a success and all that. Well, so what? I mean, it is satisfying, it gives you a charge. But once you have done that, perhaps it is not so important. I had quite a few friends who had babies at the same time as me, who were not in the women's movement. They were professional women at the BBC, or in University lecturing, who had late children at about thirty-eight or so. They had been in careers for eight or ten years, and they had written books and produced programmes, and when they had their babies they didn't feel at all as frenetic as I did. They tried to keep their jobs going for a while, then they gradually let them slow down. For them it was time to think of a change.

'Whereas, you see, I hadn't had a career. I hadn't had that measure of independence, or measure of success in terms of achieving what I wanted. It was much more important for me to keep both going. Now, having done both I know what has given me the most pleasure, and that is the children. But then they might not have been such a pleasure if I had given up work for them . . .'

Anna reckons that feminism has had less influence on how people arrange their domestic lives than it might, to some extent because women have been slightly afraid to take on the responsibility of being an equal breadwinner, or a main breadwinner. 'It is the husband's job that ultimately comes first. Maybe it is the more stable, maybe it is the higher paid, maybe you don't think about it very much, or maybe it is just because you don't want to be the one on whom that primary responsibility rests – given that there has to be one stable bread-earner per family. Even with us, I know that if we decided to move, I wouldn't want to be the one who got the job first. I would want Peter to get the job, and then I would see what I could get.

'I don't like the word housewife. I never really use it, and I can understand why women would feel a bit diffident and embarrassed about using it. The women who cling to it probably do so because they haven't conceived of an alternative. There is a slight back lash at the moment; a feeling that there *ought* to be some degree of status attached to being a housewife. This is a very difficult time to establish patterns with confidence. You are undermined one way or another. Either you are undermined by your child's behaviour which is not advertisement for your patterns, or by the ideology that you read or by the attitudes of your peers.

'What do you do once you have raised women's consciousness? Where do you leave them? How does it apply to their lives? All that debate and talking made a whole generation of women very miserable and *castrated* because they couldn't do anything without agonizing terribly over it, so they lost the capacity, I think, to enjoy life. Women expected instant gratification by taking a job – breaking the shackles, so to speak. And the whole Superwoman thing among my friends here frightens me. I had a friend who was going to have her first baby alone and she had to go in for high blood pressure. She sent me a card, "Superwoman didn't make it". She thought she ought to be able to manage everything, control everything. There is an interesting parallel with the Sheila Kitzinger natural childbirth thing, which made many women feel inadequate, but that is minor compared to this now, I think. Natural childbirth was the big let down being talked about five years ago. Now it is the being-able-to-manage-all-facets-of-life thing. And it is instant gratification, a short term way of seeing things that keeps coming out. The test is whether you can actually manage to stay on top, and if you find you can't and you aren't superwoman, however it is being popularly defined, then that is the bigger let down. We have moved from one to another and that is one of the biggest shifts. I don't think it is talked about enough. I think it is something most women suffer quite privately.

The Fuller balance has been worked for, but it has also grown out of the quality of their feeling for each other: 'When we got married Peter was already a lecturer; I typed his thesis. Fortunately we changed together. That's luck, isn't it? We could equally have gone different ways. Or when I wanted to do something myself Peter might not have been able to make adjustment. But we have a very strong relationship.

'I still am very much a model among certain people. I find this quite a strain. I am not saying this in any way to seem praiseworthy but it is a strain, because I feel that if I let things go then quite a lot of people are going to feel let down. In the States, all the women graduate students keep taking me out for lunch. They are just mind-boggled because all the women they know who have kept going in the field have deprived themselves of say, marriage and children, or they have given up, and had their families and children and stopped lecturing and stopped doing research. These are the two extremes which these graduate students see themselves faced with. It's what I saw over here, and it's what all my friends saw. So many say that I am the only person who seems to make it work. I make it work, but at some cost. I mean, I am not trying to maintain any fronts, there are some costs.'

Looking ahead, Anna said that she didn't know what would become of her family pattern, although she knew that a new balance was being worked out. 'Peter has reached a point where we realize that he can't do any more; so I have to do more. So I am considering working part-time. The second child and the increased demands of a child at school make this a necessity.'

Looking back, she could not help noting that the sharing pattern had much more glory in it for her husband than for herself. People tended, she said, to admire him and sympathize with him and tell her how lucky she was. Nobody thought that what *she* was doing was that remarkable.

Part Four

Conclusion: Each Other's Keeper?

> In all these struggles the harder, because the pettier, part falls on us women. While the men are invigorated by the fight in the world outside strengthened by coming face to face with the enemy, we sit at home and darn stockings. It does not banish care, and the little day to day worries slowly but surely sap one's vitality.
>
> > Letter from Jenny Marx, wife of Karl, written at the
> > age of fifty-eight.

> O my sisters, and my brothers too, soon you will be dead. Is this the way you want to live?
>
> > Fay Weldon *Remember Me* (1976)

Ten years ago Germaine Greer ended *The Female Eunuch* with a question. 'What,' she asked British women, '*will* you do?' Her italics carried a double emphasis. What were women going to do in practical terms to improve, or even revolutionize, their condition? And what, perhaps more importantly, did they have in the way of wills of their own?

The question was preceded by a whole catalogue of exhortations which made Greer's own hopes and beliefs clear : 'Women *must* (my italics this time) reject their role as principal consumers in the capitalist state. The old process *must* (again, my italics) be made new, not broken!

'The married woman *must* fight the guilt of failure in an impossible set up and examine the set up. She *must* ignore interested descriptions of her health and morality and her sexuality and assess them for herself. She *must* know her enemies. The doctors, psychiatrists and social workers and marriage guidance counsellors, priests, health visitors and popular moralists. She *must* analyse her buying habits, her day to day evasions and dishonesties, her sufferings and her real feelings towards her children, her past and her future.'

In 1974, in the conclusion of *Housewife*, Ann Oakley's riveting study of British domesticity, there were three more 'musts' which the author saw as preconditions of any real change for women : 'The Housewife role must be abolished. The family must be abolished. Gender roles must be abolished.'

On the first count, she declared that 'Housework is work directly opposed to the possibility of self-actualization.' (Which, put another way, means that housework gets in the way of women doing their own thing.) On point two she declares 'women's domesticity is a circle of learned deprivation and induced subjugation : a circle decisively centred on family life.' On the third count, she calls for an 'ideological revolution' which would abolish gender completely :

'Only when men *en masse* are refusing to worry about the size and strength of their erections, about their careers and their earning powers and their cars, when they cease to think of women as bitchy creatures to be put upon as aesthetic and sexual objects for the decoration of the environment and the masculine ego, when they cease to bond with other men at football matches and in pubs while women wash dishes and are denied any media interest in *their* world will something actually be happening to gender roles.'

She also suggests a small practical step women might take : they should consciously teach their daughters *not* to do housework and their sons how to do it. (The mind boggles at the family rows that would spring from this kind of positive discrimination.)

I quote Greer and Oakley at length because they are two of the best known, and indeed the best, of the many women who have been writing about the feminine condition and what should be done about it in the past ten years. The fervour of their imperatives has been echoed by other feminists both in books and in the press and on television. Perhaps their sense of urgency has, on the whole, been replaced by less declamatory prose, more pragmatic schemes and campaigns. The sex discrimination legislation was an obvious milestone, and a lot of energy was expended in getting it through; there is still, at the time of writing, plenty required for the defence of women's rights under the Abortion Act of 1967. Agitation for day care for under fives, and other such vital issues for women, bubble away, erupting occasionally (although under the Thatcher axe, the last mentioned looks an even more forlorn hope than ever).

But what of the 'ideological revolution' itself? Last summer Ann Oakley wrote despairingly in *New Society* about the lack of progress towards equality. 'Recent reforms' she said 'have only scratched the surface of women's unequal treatment.' Why? 'The cure has failed to work simply because the disease has been wrongly diagnosed.'

At the core of this misdiagnosis, she argued, was the notion that only by raising women's status and participation in the 'outside' world would equality be achieved. It was because of this that legal equality, control of fertility, employment participation and political activity have been the main areas tackled. Oakley examined the progress made in these and was, rightly, not impressed by what she found.

The rising number of married women at work outside the home (from 42 per cent in 1971 to 50 per cent in 1978) for instance: 'It is widely regarded as an important index of something, though nobody knows quite what.' Most of them, she pointed out, have gone into part time work or into the traditional areas of female employment. They are, therefore, the lowest paid workers; many are unemployed. There is still only a tiny proportion of women in top jobs.

It all comes back to the old difficulty: 'The double burden of women is not resolved by legislative directives about equal pay, equal employment, opportunity, sex discrimination in education, and so on because these do not alter the responsibilities women have for domestic work and child rearing. Men and women cannot be equal partners outside the home if they are not equal partners inside it.' Which turns the other egalitarian argument – that women will only achieve equality if they have it outside the home – on its head. What Ann Oakley did not write but might have is that the 'outside equality first' argument is a deeply divisive one among women themselves.

A whole generation of post-Suffragette women grew up believing that they somehow had to choose: if they wanted a career in the professions they must abandon thoughts of family life and children, and vice versa. It is only very recently, within the last twenty years, in fact, that middle class and 'further educated' women have taken on the kind of load working class women have, as we have seen, carried for generations. But these 'superwomen' have been, in many cases, cut off from their sisters who have opted for, or got caught in, a more traditional one-sided domestic situation. Thus the bitter arguments about motherhood, and whether or not a child should be parted from his or her mother for the first few years of life, are often to do with one woman envying another's 'freedom'. The resentment of the woman whose husband thinks that one Laura Ashley dress and a change of denim dungarees is all that she needs by way of wardrobe, when she sees the clothes and sparkle (however spurious) of a woman who earns her own money and can afford more variety is understandable, but tragic.

Which 'type' of women do men prefer? The cosy homemaker (smouldering with rage as she dishes up the stew or irons the shirts) or the worldly success (yearning for family life, or struggling as she tries to combine it with a job that isn't so glamorous as it looks from the kitchen sink)? A woman who is a housewife and also a playwright told me that men have often flirted with her over the dinner table with such blandishments as 'how I wish my wife were more like you ... you are so interesting.' Only to follow up, at a later stage in the conversation with, 'if you were my wife, I'd soon lick you into shape.'

Because of men's divisive tactics and their eagerness to play one 'type' of woman off against another, women must be forgiven for their own defensive response. But the split between women (not to mention between men and women) might narrow a lot if men simply took on more household responsibility. Housework would not get in the way of self actualization if it were something everyone took a hand in. I don't mean just the husband doing the dishes, but definitely assuming joint responsibility with his wife for keeping the joint home running. Women would have to give up a little territory (even women who hate housework seem to see it as somehow linked to power) and men would have to give up a little time in the pub or club or wherever. If it were generally acknowledged that husbands had a joint domestic role apart from mending fuses and mowing the grass, then employers would have to take it into consideration too.

There is some evidence that this is beginning to happen. As women in employment increasingly strike good deals over maternity leave and can more freely request time off to deal with domestic crises without the heavens or productivity falling, men are seeing that there could be a better balance between work and 'real life'; there are other priorities. They aren't doing it *en masse* yet but another ten years may see a dramatic change here. I am sure Ann Oakley is right to say that she knows of no good evidence that women's share of the domestic responsibilities has fallen in ten years. But I simply cannot agree with her that 'housework hours have risen because standards have risen.' Before the war I have already pointed out, servants put in horrifically long hours doing the housework for the richer families; the poorer wives, as Margery Spring Rice's Committee found as late as 1939, often worked a fifteen or sixteen hour day in their own homes without any respite, or cultural diversion – not even television advertising.

The average number of pregnancies among these women was five; and it was 'the cumulative effect of years of ever-increasing toil which, even if it results in no definite disease, crushes the vitality of so many working mothers and reduces them too often by the age of forty or fifty to a grievous and irremediable state of health.' It was 'often heartbreaking to see how rapidly a pretty, attractive girl grows old and drab after a few years of marriage. She loses her looks and ceases to take pride in her appearance; minor ailments are neglected, her temper is frayed and household worries weigh unnecessarily heavy.'

Forty years on, Ann Oakley still gets to the crux when she asks why participation in the outside world was seen as the right way to go about getting sexual equality between the sexes. 'One reason why women should become like men is that if men become like women their status is threatened rather than women's raised,' she can see.

But if women move outside the home they put themselves in male hands in another way . . . thus the no-win situation Oakley

211

so despairs about. She calls roundly for a reappraisal of ideas of what sex equality is. At the moment, women can't win 'because they have to choose between two destinies, a feminine and a masculine. No legislation for sex equality can be effective if it fails to tackle the difference between the 'natural sex differences and the social and domestic roles.'

She may be right, but it is in precisely this kind of argument that the women's movement loses recruits. Women on the whole do not want to give up the hope of some expression of their own sexuality, their own gender difference is precious to them. They have found being forced to ape men painful enough; persuading men to become more like them may be more threatening still.

Here we come close to the greatest failure of feminism: it has so far not been able to offer a really convincing alternative to the warmth of a conventional family situation when it works well. And women may do well to beware of promises of independence and sisterhood as a substitute for it.

In *The Broken Heart*, James J. Lynch's chilling study of 'the medical consequences of loneliness' he shows how heart disease is discernibly greater among bereaved, divorced, lonely people, and how the cliche of the nurse's healing hand on the brow really *is* a factor in restoring health. Human physical contact is vital for mental and physical health – a simple truth, but one we have not valued highly enough in the age of independence.

Feminists argue that women can sustain each other. Fine, up to a point, or if they are lesbian, but what if not? The need for close physical contact between mother and child is now recognized and encouraged. Stroking and holding and cuddling help the mother and the child thrive. For adults there has been more concentration on technique, on satisfaction, on climax. Is women's concentration on their right to orgasm merely another version of the male anxiety about the 'size and strength of his erections'?

'Our inability to live together' is, says Lynch, one of the central facts that seems to cause us to die prematurely. He goes on to quote the deadly statistics and shows a clear relationship between premature death and emotional-physical deprivation. 'It is a striking fact that US mortality rates for all causes of death

212

and not just heart disease are consistently higher for divorced, single and widowed individuals of both sexes and all races. Some of the increased death rates in unmarried individuals are astounding, rising as high as ten times the rates for married people of comparable ages.'

He castigates the new insistence on independence which he sees as a chimera. Perhaps instead women should be seeking new patterns of interdependence to avoid what Jill Tweedie called in her recent book *In The Name Of Love* the 'glue of dependency' and endeavour to relate to each other freely and equally.

Lynch's thesis may be no great argument for marriage's ecstatic happiness in the rosy, romantic happy-ever-after sense. It may simply be that boredom and cosiness are healthier and safer than tortured singleness, where great passion or love if it comes at all, is accompanied by terrible fears of loss, and long patches of being alone, face to face with oneself. But surely it is the flaws in the economic and social system that make marriage so boring, so difficult to sustain – it is not the basic notion of two people of opposite, or should we say, complementary, sex living together and having children, that is at fault. Most of the married or cohabiting women in this book have turned their back on any overt feminism because deep in their hearts they want a good human relationship with a man more than they want even Erin Pizzey's three piece suite.

To defend marriage or at least 'pair bonding' is not to defend people living in little self-contained boxes . . . that is as dangerous as the notion of individual independence. But the women's movement will not, I fear, achieve its objective of the ending of female servitude, both inside the home and outside it, until it recognizes that men and women need each other. They will have to educate their brothers as well as their sisters and try to find a new rapprochement. There are signs of a move towards this. Young couples today, according to research carried out for advertising agencies, enter marriage full of ideals about sharing and mutual support. But too often the system and the girl's conditioning about her biological role betray her later on.

As soon as you take on a role, it takes you on. If you become a mother, age twenty-four, undercurrents from ages past start tugging, and there is an inevitable retreat into the role of mum/

housewife. Many women at this stage even make a willing sacrifice of what they see as their other potential. After all, what is more important than children?

The man, likewise becomes more and more the 'husband' assuming the role of total breadwinner and therefore total boss. The places in the jigsaw are well prepared and the hapless idealistic pair slide into them. But there is nothing predetermined about it although it often looks that way. As a single parent I have played both roles and can see that, if I were the only breadwinner, I could behave like the worst of husbands. As it is I am restrained by being a woman, chastened by having to do even the minimal housework I do carry out and by having to organize and care for a child too.

The inescapable conclusion is, however, that the 'new' feminist philosophy can only be fully embraced by those women who have been hit really hard by the system: divorced women, battered women, lonely women, single parents, lesbians. These disadvantaged people form a growing chunk of the female population certainly, but not all of them have bought the feminist ticket even yet.

Most women are still in a twilight world, caught between the new 'liberated' image they are supposed to aspire to, and still held by the old benefits of being 'kept', of being in their 'proper place'.

The rousing polemic of Greer and others asked for an exercise of will and emotion greater than most women, whose difficulties were chronic rather than acute, could manage.

The trouble is as one woman told me: 'To be a feminist one needs in a way to be less than human at the beginning ... to refuse to do things which might be regarded only as common kindness, to refuse to provide services previously taken for granted.'

Many women we spoke to had been alienated by the *image* of feminism (some of which can of course be blamed on the antics of the male dominated media). They saw it as po-faced, anti-men, too left wing, and above all anti what they liked about themselves. The women's magazines score because, however, spuriously, they seem to offer a possibility of a prettier, better, more competent self. It is hard to get women to follow you *en masse*

214

if you ask them to throw off not just the chains of domestic servitude but the trappings which had made the servitude bearable till now – make up, self adornment, men themselves. Of course it is not a feminist rule that women must make themselves plain, but many women vaguely imagine it is. What is closer to the truth is that, to begin with, feminists abandoned conventional decoration because it seemed to be only dedicated to men the predators, and to the perpetuation of a cosmetics and fashion industry that also preyed upon women's anxieties about their sexual attractiveness. There was also a kind of freedom, some thought, it in the sexual anonymity of baggy dungarees and frizzy hair. (Things have relaxed a lot now and the fashion industry itself has borrowed and learned from feminism.)

There are other fears: one woman felt that to be in favour of women's lib in any overt way would somehow rob her of her children (it would be necessary for her to work) as well as her comfort (she lived in a comfortable, but not plush, suburban house) and her husband (she didn't 'get on' with him in any deep spiritual way and found sex with him 'boring' but he was 'kind' and they were 'used to each other now'). The abyss that any shaking of this structure would open would be too much for her and probably not worth it. She, like others, still had romantic dreams hovering at the back of her mind of a career, a great love, some sort of vague freedom, but she was pinning those increasingly on her children.

Another woman talked of the 'shell' of suburban life, rather in the manner of one of Betty Friedan's case histories: 'It's so repetitive. The women say goodbye to their husbands in the morning, they look after the children and clean the house and talk to each other, if they are lucky. The kids trail round after them with bits of blanket and bottles, whining. Then the husbands come home and they eat and watch television and it goes on and on. Few of the women have any confidence left, although many are well educated and trained. It is a world without much danger physically except the harm you can do with tranquillizers or in playgrounds. But it lacks stimulation and exposure to anything the women can perceive as *real*. Those who say they know they are doing "the most important job", which is bringing up the children and that makes them happy, are lying to protect their own self respect. It's better than moaning and doing nothing.'

Another even told of the pitfalls in the babysitting points system. There were meetings, copied from male establishment goings-on, where one member accused another of fudging the figures (no money is involved, only time); one woman was banned from the circle because she was 'on valium'. On the other hand this woman *loved* babysitting itself: 'It's the only chance I get to do the reading, television-watching and other things that I really want to do. If I were in my own house I'd be ironing or cooking or something.'

So, the captive wife still lives and the domestic dilemma still remains unsolved. Giving a woman a job outside the home, as Ann Oakley says, too often simply doubles her burden because her housework and service role continue in tandem. If this is liberation then all that has happened that women are jumping out of the frying pan into the fire. There will be (*pace* Shirley Conran and the advertising agencies) no race of Superwomen fit to cope with 'success' abroad and 'housework' at home. The Selma James solution does not seem to go far enough – it would take a hell of a lot of Wages for Housework to liberate the average housewife. Those who argue that such payment would simply confirm women in their traditional role are probably right.

What we should fight for is a situation whereby no one person 'keeps' another. Perhaps, in the age of the much vaunted microchip, men will be forced to reclaim some domestic responsibility in order to give themselves enough to do. Or perhaps they will realize that the system under which they work now is inhuman and turns them into emotionally deprived, if materially indulged, androids.

What is often forgotten is that it is not women's fault, nor even the fault of their husbands, that women's participation in the commercial 'outside' world is so difficult to combine with the interests of the family and children. It is still very squarely the fault of a system which imposes a rigid and cruel division between work and home, and thus widens the division between men and women. Various women with very different points of view have agreed in the pages of this book that somehow housework and staying at home generally should be given greater status and financial reward.

That, alone, would not solve the problem and might exacerbate it; there *is* no exclusively feminine destiny, and in a capitalist, cost effective society, it is very hard for anyone to feel really part of the world unless she – or he – spends some working hours outside their own four walls. Women have scarcely begun to get a foothold 'outside'; it seems madness to push women 'back home' when most have never got out in the first place. What we should surely be fighting for is greater flexibility, the right to move from one to the other as the need and desire arises. A few years at home, or working part time, is attractive, provided you don't wake up every morning in a panic thinking 'I'll never work again' or 'I'm stuck for life'. And men could do with some domestic 'humanizing' just as women lack worldly experience.

However, this book, although it has hinged on the emergence of the new feminism, was never intended, and does not in any sense claim to be, a history of the women's movement of the seventies. It was not written in any spirit of judgement either – it is much too early for that and I'm not qualified to do it anyhow. What I have been interested to do is trace the outer ripples of the movement's influence and to ask why, when so many of the feminist arguments are so clearly stated with such cogency, and when there is not a single woman in the country who has not heard at least some of them, even if only in a garbled version, there has been so little radical change in the structure of things. Has the movement failed? Was it destined to be of help to the few while the mainstream go merrily, or miserably, on as before? Will the generation of girls now coming to maturity be the sisters of tomorrow? Or will they again fall for the blandishments or moralists and advertisers who daily reinforce the validity of a domestic destiny – with whatever else it may be combined?

There was only space to tell a few women's stories in full, and, as must be obvious, I have written in detail about women who face no particularly dramatic difficulty in their lives, no especial handicap – although some have special advantages such as money or education. One way or another they are mostly women who live in the mainstream – they live with men and enjoy the traditional pleasures of family life even if aware that these are fragile. Alongside them I have cited the views and recounted the theories and suggestions of some of those who feel they have answers to problems even the happiest 'housewife' faces now : problems which chiefly centre around the wish for 'self actualization' plus a home and a family and a man as well. This has been traditionally thought of as a middle class woman's 'wanting everything' difficulty. But it must be obvious from these interviews that it crosses the class barrier, and applies to all income groups. Whether it is the women's movement which has raised consciousness to this level, or whether it is better education and economic conditions and fewer children that has combined with feminism to do so, is a matter for debate.

I could have chosen to tell the stories of women *in extremis* and there are still plenty of those in Britain now. Thanks to the women's movement and the activities of certain groups and individuals, they now have a better chance of getting a hearing if not a settlement. We may not have a more compassionate society than before but it is at least easier to raise a voice or a standard. And there are plenty of causes : there are women who have become more and more alienated in the ten years past, women who have been failed by their husbands or children or doctors; the growing number of alcoholics, the women on valium and other tranquillizers (there were 20 million prescriptions for sedatives and tranquillizers in Britain in 1978 – most of them for women).

There are women with depression, there are women on the bread line much as in the days of Margery Spring Rice, although now tussling with the fine print of the social security system. They get a meagre benefit, but live in constant fear that a spy will report their 'cohabitation' with a man and they will lose even that. It is a sad reflection on a society that has endorsed, if not liberation, some notion of equality, that the poorest women should be subjected to a system that seems designed to keep them poor and isolated. If a woman on supplementary benefit, which aims merely to keep her and her children alive, attempts to get back into the mainstream by getting a job (probably low paid and part time) or loving a man, she has the 'benefit' immediately curtailed or removed. In the latter case the man, whether he is a bounder or a beggar, is regarded as the legal supporter of the woman simply by virtue of the fact that he lives under the same roof. (This is unfair on men too of course, but that is another story.)

Single parents at all levels, whether divorced or unmarried, are still discriminated against as are their children – although I believe the next ten years will see a dramatic change in that as the numbers grow and there are more single fathers. (I should declare an interest here. I am a single parent who has suffered the very minimum of discrimination. With friendly employers, adequate maternity leave, helpful friends and neighbours, a lonely situation was better for me than for most others I know in similar condition. What my son will have to face has yet to be seen.)

The iniquity of the tax system will take many years to unravel from its devotion to the notion of man as breadwinner and woman as dependant or pin money spinner.

I have quoted black women without identifying their race but have not attempted any assessment of the Asian or West Indian communities, although in many cases they suffer the worst our society has to offer. The Asian women's case and condition was movingly and intimately portrayed by Amrit Wilson in her book *Finding a Voice*, published by Virago in 1978. West Indian women have not suffered the same cultural alienation and indeed have brought some very positive exuberant values with them into our society – real *love* of children, an ability to celebrate, a strong family sense which has nothing at all to do with our narrow nuclear family. They have however suffered double discrimination in employment – both because they are black and because they are women. What happens to their daughters now growing up will be a good way to measure whether white society has any intention of ever admitting black people to a proper share of running what is now their own country.

Good things *have* happened in ten years. There is less humbug about women; in spite of media clichés the language used both by us and about us is less coy, less abusive. Both less and more is expected of us. The young single woman now has an ease, a freedom, she sometimes doesn't appreciate because she has known little else. The hard-eyed teenagers who state so confidently their own demands and expectations may have a shock coming when they succumb to the old order and marry and have children; but they will probably fight back more quickly than their mothers.

The 'person' joke, much bandied at the time of the Sex Discrimination legislation, has gone. 'Ms' has become a more or less accepted form of address and designation, even by officialdom. 'Feminist' is increasingly a label with its own British rather than borrowed American identity, and is being used by women who might never attend a meeting or join a campaign. There are women who will, like some interviewed earlier in this book, deny all interest in 'women's lib' but in the same breath express solid support for the main feminist issues – especially some form of equality between the sexes at work and in the home. Women have learned to stand up for themselves against violence from the State and from men. Confidence is growing.

In spite of the PM and the Queen sticking to stuffy formality in dress, women's looks and clothes have been revolutionized. Since the mini, the last restrictive mass fashion 'look', it has been possible for a woman to wear more or less what she feels like. Denims and dungarees can be smart or sloppy; they are worn by men and women alike. A leading feminist told me that, to begin with in the movement, women had used denims for anonymity, as a way to diminish the kind of sexuality society demanded of them. Now there is greater confidence and the anonymous look has a cachet and an appeal of its own. But in the past few seasons there has been what some have seen as a rather sinister return to a more tailored corseted look: bras and suspender belts are photographed as if from an American magazine of the fifties even on the *Guardian* women's page. The same page recently asked a woman returning to work after caring for two children at home for five years to choose clothes: she flung off her denims in exchange for a boring tailored suit and a silk blouse tied in a knot at the neck – the trad boardroom image.

The danger for a teenager, or young woman, now seems to me that, with all her new confidence and freedom, she will fall even more readily for the over romantic view of marriage. I have listened with sinking heart as a twenty-one year old proudly showed me her sumptuous wedding album – a candle-lit, soft-focus picture of her veiled self on the cover and every detail of the day's ritual caught in full colour inside. All for £150. She bloomed with the time-honoured radiance as she described the presents and good wishes she and her new, rather silent and shuffling husband had been given. They were of course going to share everything equally, and she was going to go on working. No problem. Children? They wanted at least three but that could wait. What will happen when they do come?

Time will tell, but I have some inkling that one reason why girls still 'under achieve' in their later years at school is that they still, whatever egalitarian notions have got through to them, believe a man will take care of them from age twenty-three onwards. Thus they sell themselves short for training and employment first time around, and when it comes to a return to work after having been through the mill of child bearing and rearing, there is nothing but part time or low paid servitude of the kind they do at home anyway on offer. However, *Spare Rib* reports that many schoolgirls are now buying the magazine as 'their own' magazine. Let us hope they are taking in the warnings so liberally sprinkled on its pages.

Other worthier writers have come up with programmes for action for women. I only want to repeat one suggestion, after listening to hours of women talking about themselves. This is that the word 'housewife' be struck from the record; that it should no longer be permissible to write it on forms or acceptable as self-description in any other place. It both demeans and deludes women, and it also enables them to cop out of responsibility for themselves or a broader commitment to the community. It isolates men by cutting down their responsibility for the home to a minimum. It is no longer a proper job description. One of the maddening things about housework whether it is washing the clothes or doing all those little caring services like sending birthday cards to mother-in-law, is that it is repetitive and could be done by anyone. And children are not a good enough excuse for dumping it all onto one partner.

If men and women live together under contract and decide to

share children, then share them they should. At the moment child care and housework are lumped together, but they should not be. If a woman decides to stay at home, or has to stay at home while her children are small because her husband's earning power is greater than hers and anywhere there is no reliable form of day care to let her out, then that is what she stays at home for. Obviously the bulk of the housework will fall on her at that time, but *all* of it need not. No excuses from men about a hard day at the office making it impossible to take on some home management should be accepted. Anyone who has both spent hard days in the office and hard days looking after one or more children will tell you which is the more exhausting.

Also, the child care should be seen very clearly for what it is – a temporary commitment. Even if a woman devotes ten or more years to it exclusively, it will end. All-day commitment ends much sooner, unless children are very widely spaced and all the trends are against that. Employers, the State and women themselves should recognize the necessity of keeping a woman in touch with the outside world, and of keeping it in touch with her, for the benefit of both. The more the 'housewife' is required to give some of her time to acquiring and maintaining out-of-home or applied skills, the more she will know that society expects more of her than selfish domesticity and dedicated motherhood. She will respond better, and have a better opinion of herself.

To achieve this, there would have to be an end to the man's total control of money. If he opts for a wife and children, then what he earns is for him and for them especially if there is a period when the woman cannot or does not wish to earn. Many men recognize this and give their wives 'everything they want'. That isn't the point; such generosity could stop at a stroke and creates terrible dependence. Even the divorce law, which seems to offer women security in that she is 'likely to get' the family home, is unsatisfactory. It is punitive on a man and not much good to a helpless woman. There may be a kind of poetic justice in the situation where a woman who has married for a three-piece suite and a nice house in Ruislip ends up with a three-piece suite and a house in Ruislip, but it is not what we should be aiming for.

Some scheme should be devised whereby the earnings in a family are divided all along. I don't just mean a joint bank account to which a woman is given free access. I mean that half the man's salary – in the situation where the man is earning and the woman is not – should be paid direct to the woman for her to dispense as she pleases or thinks fit. There would be certain pre-agreed areas where expenses would be split – mortgages, rent and so on.

There are a million pitfalls here, and versions would have to be devised for different income groups and styles of living, but it would be a stunning blow for *machismo* and would revolutionize the marriage system. Perhaps the service could be rewritten. Instead of the hypocritical 'With *all* my worldly goods I thee endow' it should read 'With half our worldly goods we endow each other'.

Under this situation a man might refuse to meet his commitments to the children or go off and spend half on marauding. But at least the woman would have *something* of her own. If it were taxed separately as her income, better still. This is pipe dreaming of course, but I trust that similar pipe dreams will continue to be floated during the 1980s and that *Spare Rib*'s assurance that there are more and more self help and consciousness raising groups springing up at a low-profile, grass-roots level is true. Even though there is a deeply conventional streak in our society that is clinging to the system which seems to offer the least danger and the minimum of loneliness, it is letting women down too often now for the romance to hold much longer.

The last ten years or so have been hard for women: the next may be even harder. But even women who have been through very black times indeed find it possible, on the edge of the eighties, to summon optimism. One, who has been through a bitter divorce which left her with three children to bring up alone and almost penniless, looks back to the so-called swinging sixties with horror. Recently her daughter organized a 'sixties party' and Mum produced a Biba mini dress for her to wear. The sixteen year old tried it on and said 'Ugh, how could you ever have worn it, Mummy.' 'I wondered too,' said her mother, who found the entire party macabre in the extreme. 'When I watched them all twisting, dressed up in the clothes I and my friends had worn, I felt suddenly overwhelmed with the misery that I had felt then: the conformism and the insistence that all was well. I remembered how depressed I had been, and yet if anyone had suggested I was less than happily married, I would not have known what they were talking about. My husband used to say, "What's the matter with you? Why are you so depressed?" It drove him mad, but there was never any suggestion that it might be something to do with him. I didn't *know* he was having lots of affairs.

'Now I am alone altogether and I'd prefer not to be, but I'm altogether more at ease about being a woman: I think that the women who come after us will still have to fight terribly hard; but at least it is agreed that we are fighting for the right things.'

Index